WEST INDIAN READERS

BOOK THREE

D1638189

ODYSSEUS LEAVING THE GIANTS' ISLE. (*See Lesson 15.*)

NELSON'S

WEST INDIAN READERS

Book THREE

Compiled by J. O. Cutteridge

NELSON THORNES

First edition published in 1926 by Thomas Nelson & Sons, with subsequent revisions.

This edition published in 2013 by:
Nelson Thornes Ltd
Delta Place
27 Bath Road
CHELTENHAM
GL53 7TH
United Kingdom

13 14 15 16 17 / 10 9 8 7 6 5 4 3 2

A catalogue record for this book is available from the British Library

ISBN 978 1 4085 2354 4

Page make-up by Compuscript Ltd
Printed by Multivista Global Ltd

PREFATORY NOTE FOR TEACHERS

THIS Book has been prepared on a similar plan to the first two of the series. Teachers are again advised to read the Prefatory Note in Book I. on the aims of the Readers and the method of treatment to be followed.

The elementary lessons on "Health" in Book II. have been developed by additional lessons in this Book, leading to a simple presentation of two of the most common of tropical diseases—viz. hookworm and malaria. I am indebted to Dr. J. R. Dickson, Deputy Surgeon-General, Trinidad, for assistance in this section of the work.

The treatment of lessons on plant life and natural history is intentionally of a general character, and is not designed to supplant Nature-Study lessons, but rather to supply reading-matter as a basis for a more scientific treatment in that sphere.

The literature given in this Book should be supplemented by the following books:—

1. *Stories from the Odyssey.* Nelson's "Told to the Children" Series.

2. *Stories from the Iliad.* Nelson's "Told to the Children" Series.

3. *Stories of King Arthur's Knights.* Nelson's "Told to the Children" Series.

4. *Martin Rattler.* Nelson's Classics.

5. *Twenty Thousand Leagues under the Sea.* Collins' "Pocket Classics."

6. *Kingsley's Heroes.* Nelson's "Teaching of English" Series.

7. *Tanglewood Tales.* Hawthorne. Nelson's "Teaching of English" Series.

My thanks are due, and are hereby tendered, to Sir Francis Watts, K.C.M.G., D.Sc., for kindly reading the proofs of Books I., II., and III., and for the very valuable suggestions and criticisms he has offered; to Judge Russell for permission to utilize two of his poems from *The Legends of the Bocas*; to Mr. L. O. Inniss for the Creole Folk-Tale; as well as to all others who have assisted in any way with the preparation of this book.

J. O. Cutteridge

Acknowledgements

The author and the publisher would also like to thank the following for permission to reproduce material:

Text Permissions
p200: reproduced with permission of the poet's grandson Roger Squire; p205–6: reprinted by permission of The Society of Authors as the Literary Representative of the Estate of John Masefield.

Images
p1: Ulysses Deriding Polyphemus, 1829 (oil on canvas) (for detail see 99614), Turner, Joseph Mallord William (1775–1851)/National Gallery, London, UK/The Bridgeman Art Library; p19: Frank C. Pape; p.30 British Museum; pp36–37: Mr. PL Guppy (Trinidad); p47: Picturebank/Alamy; p48: Edward Fielding/Shutterstock; p49: Photos12/Alamy; p53: Sons of the Brave, 1880 (oil on canvas), Morris, Philip Richard (1838–1902)/Leeds Museums and Galleries (Leeds Art Gallery) U.K./The Bridgeman Art Library; p62: Mr. PL Guppy (Trinidad); p72: John E. Satelille; p79: Universal Image Group Ltd/Alamy; p91: Garry Gay/Getty Images; p94: Foodfolio/Alamy; p95: Diane MacDonald/Alamy; p105: W. Heath-Robinson; p109: Bloomberg/Getty Images; p111: Fancoise de Valera/Alamy; p112: RGB Ventures/DBA/Superstock; p113: James Davies; p116: The Horse that Destroyed a City, illustration from 'The Hero Legends', 1962 (gouache on paper), Embleton, Gerry (b.1941)/Private Collection/© Look and Learn/The Bridgeman Art Library; p124: The Crown Estate/Bridgeman Art Library; p130: Ian Wood/Alamy; p133: Corbis; p167: Pete Niesen/Alamy; p174: The passing of King Arthur, illustration from 'Stories of Legendary Heroes' (colour litho), Brock, Henry Matthew (1875–1960)/Private Collection/The Bridgeman Art Library; p180(L): Gaertner/Alamy; p180(R): Elizabeth Leyden/Alamy; p189: Innes Fripp; p191: Beryl Peters/Alamy.

Every effort has been made to trace the copyright holders but if any have been inadvertently overlooked the publisher will be pleased to make the necessary arrangements at the first opportunity.

CONTENTS

An Asterisk (*) indicates Poetry.

LESSON 1

THE WEST INDIES

YOU have already read of many of the other West Indian islands besides your own, but perhaps you do not know exactly where they are. This lesson will help you to form a clear idea of what we mean by the West Indies and the place of each island in the group.

Look at the map on page 10, and you will see a long chain of islands stretching in a big curve from North America to South America. They have been called a necklace of precious pearls strung across the ocean from Florida to Venezuela.

The West Indies is the general name for this archipelago or mass of islands, which extends across the entrance to the Caribbean Sea. It consists of a large number of islands and islets, some of which are mere rocks, and may be divided into three main groups, the Greater Antilles, the Lesser Antilles, and the Bahamas.

The Greater Antilles are the group which contains the largest islands: Cuba, Hispaniola, Jamaica, and Puerto Rico.

The Lesser Antilles form a string of much smaller islands reaching from the east of Puerto Rico to within seven miles of the South American coast. They are divided into two smaller groups,

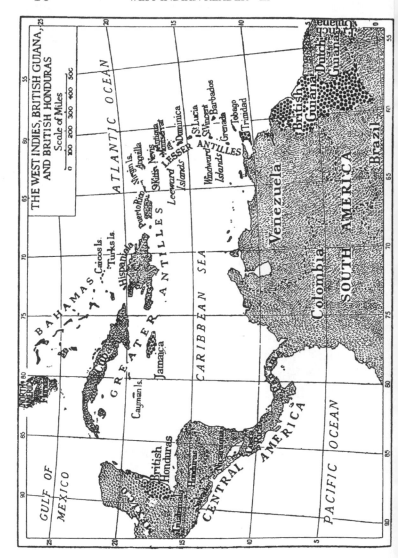

the Leeward Islands to the north and the Windward Islands to the south.

The Bahamas, north of Cuba, form a chain of coral islands and banks or reefs extending for many hundred miles in a direction from north-west to south-east. They include Guanahani or Watling Island, which was the first land of the New World discovered by Columbus.

The largest islands, Cuba, Hispaniola, and Puerto Rico, form part of Latin America—that is, the lands which were discovered, conquered, and settled by the Spaniards and Portuguese, both of which are Latin races.

Jamaica, the Bahamas, and most of the Lesser Antilles became British possessions. They fell into six groups—(1) Jamaica, with Turks, Caicos, and Cayman Islands; (2) the Bahamas; (3) the Leeward Islands; (4) the Windward Islands; (5) Barbados; (6) Trinidad and Tobago. In 1958 all these islands except group (2) combined to form the British Caribbean Federation. In 1962 Britain dissolved this Federation after groups (1) and (6) withdrew. Other islands are governed by France, Holland, or the United States.

There were two British colonies on the mainland in the region of the West Indies, as you can see on the map. They were Belize on the Yucatan peninsula in Central America, and Guyana the only British colony on the mainland of South America. The latter was often spoken of in the West Indies as Demerara,

but this is really the name of only one province
in that country.

Now study the following list very carefully,
and find each island on the map:—

Islands and Colonies.	Area in square miles.	Number of people 1960.	Capital.
1. Jamaica:	4,411	1,613,000	Kingston.
The Turks and Caicos Islands.	166	5,700	Grand Turk.
The Cayman Islands.	100	7,600	George Town.
2. The Bahamas.	4,400	106,700	Nassau.
3. The Leeward Islands, including:			
(a) Antigua.	108	54,400	St. John's.
Barbuda.	62		
(b) St. Kitts.	68	38,300	Basseterre.
(c) Nevis.	155	12,800	Charlestown.
(d) Anguilla.	35	5,600	The Road.
(e) Montserrat.	32	12,200	Plymouth.
(f) The Virgin Is.	58	7,300	Roadtown.
4. The Windward Islands, including:			
(a) Grenada.	133	88,700	St. George's.
(b) St. Lucia.	238	94,700	Castries.
(c) St. Vincent.	150	80,000	Kingstown.
(d) Dominica.	290	59,100	Roseau.
5. Barbados.	166	232,100	Bridgetown.
6. Trinidad and Tobago.	1,980	826,000	Port of Spain.
7. Belize.	8,866	90,300	Belmopan.
8. Guyana.	83,000	575,300	Georgetown.

(Names of Commonwealth Islands underlined)

Exercises

1. Write out the name of each of the Commonwealth West Indies, and that of its chief town. Spell these properly.
2. Which places given in the list are not strictly "West Indies"?
3. Divide the number of people by the number of square miles in each case: this gives you the number of people to each square mile. Now arrange the names in the first column, beginning with the one which has the most people to the square mile. Perhaps your teacher will tell you why some have more than others.
4. Why do you think that French and Dutch steamers come to the West Indies?
5. Where is Demerara?
6. Draw a map showing your own island and that of its six nearest neighbours.

LESSON 2

WASPS, BUTTERFLIES, AND MOTHS

WASPS, marabuntas, or "Jack Spaniards" are a very interesting family. Some live together in large numbers, building nests on the roofs of outhouses.

Others live alone, making a row of cells of mud like little hollow balls, attached to a wall or ceiling. When the tiny home is complete and dry,

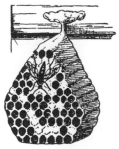

(1.) Jack Spaniard.   (2.) Nest of Jack Spaniard.

the builder goes hunting. Soon it brings back, from time to time, a small caterpillar or a spider.

Whether it be one or the other, the Jack Spaniard has stung it so cleverly that it cannot move, although it does not die. When four or five of the little victims have been put into a cell of the nest, the wasp drops an egg in, closes the entrance, and flies away.

The egg hatches, and a tiny grub appears and feasts on the caterpillars or spiders. When they are finished the grub ceases to feed.

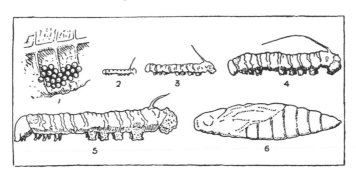

Stages in growth of Frangipani Moth.
1. Eggs; 2, 3, 4, 5, Growth of caterpillar; 6. Pupa.

Soon its form begins to change. Feelers, head, thorax, abdomen, legs, and wings gradually appear. Then it breaks open the ball or cell and crawls out as a complete insect. The sun and air soon change it to the proper colour, dry its wings, and fit it for life. Then away it flies as the Jack Spaniard you know so well, ready to sting if you attack it.

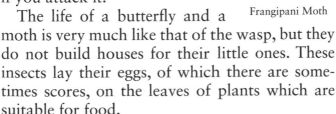

Frangipani Moth

The life of a butterfly and a moth is very much like that of the wasp, but they do not build houses for their little ones. These insects lay their eggs, of which there are sometimes scores, on the leaves of plants which are suitable for food.

When the eggs hatch, the little ones, which we call caterpillars, begin to feed on the leaves of the plant on which the eggs were laid. They go on feeding and growing until their skins get too tight. Then the skins burst, but the lucky little creatures find others, and larger ones, underneath when the old ones are thrown off. This happens several times.

At last there comes a time when the caterpillars can eat no more. Then, according to their kind, they hide either in the earth, or in some old wall, or in a hollow tree, or very often remain on the plant on which they fed.

Well-known West Indian Butterflies (reduced in size).

There some of them spin a garment for themselves which covers them all over. Others cover themselves with earth or pieces of stick and leaves. They remain quite still for a certain time, and if they are touched they move a little, but do not try to get away.

The great moment in their lives arrives when their garments burst, and out come the butterflies or moths. For some time they hardly move, but gradually they spread their wings, and when these are dry and of the proper colour the perfect insects fly away.

The two long hair-like feelers of the butterfly have thick ends like clubs. Those of the moth have pointed ends. Moths, too, lock their wings together by means of a tiny hook on the inner margin of one wing which fits into an eye on the inner margin of the other wing.

Butterflies fly by day, but most moths fly at night.

EXERCISES

1. In what ways are Jack Spaniards and butterflies alike? In what ways are they unlike?
2. In what ways are butterflies and moths alike? In what ways are they unlike?
3. Write out all the names in the lesson which refer to *one* thing only. Begin with "family, row, wall," etc.
4. Write out all the names in the lesson which mean more than one thing. Begin with "wasps, butterflies, moths," etc.
5. From paragraph 6 to the end this lesson is written in the plural—that is, it is talking of more than one butterfly or moth. Now try to write it as if it spoke of one only. Begin like this, "This insect lays its eggs, of which there are sometimes scores, on the leaf of a plant which is suitable for food" etc.
6. Make a drawing of the Jack Spaniard on page 14.
7. Do you know any of the butterflies shown? Which of them are in your school collection?

LESSON 3

PICTURE THINKING

How many people do you see in this picture?

What is taking place in the middle distance?

What can be seen in the background?

What device is shown on the shield of the knight?

Give the knight a name taken from this device.

What name is given to an undersized person like the man to the left?

What is he holding?

What relationship is there between him and the knight?

Why are the lady and the dwarf placed to the left of the picture?

Put your finger on the spot to which your gaze returns after you look at any other part. This is called the centre of interest.

What is the centre of interest in the picture?

What change would there be in the centre of interest if the lady's face were turned towards you?

Why do you think the Red Cross Knight is fighting the dragon?

Is this fight taking place at night or in the daytime? How can you tell?

If it is night, whence comes the light to fight by?

After thinking about the questions on page 18,
compose a sentence which might be printed here.

Write three paragraphs, each describing the dress of one of the people in the picture.

Try to put the story into verses. You might begin:—

> A brave and gallant knight,
>   All armed from top to toe,
> Rode out to help a maiden

— — — — — —

LESSON 4

QUEEN MAB

Introduction.—This is a poem about Queen Mab, the queen of the fairies. Shakespeare wrote a play about fairies, which perhaps one day you will read. In it he says they are so small that they can sleep inside the flowers, and are afraid of spiders and snails. In another play he says that Queen Mab comes in a carriage and drives "across men's noses as they lie asleep" This carriage is a nutshell, and the wheels are made of spiders' legs. In it she drives through men's brains, and makes them dream of all sorts of things.

In this poem, too, Queen Mab is very small, and she makes good children dream of pleasant things, and bad children dream of horrid things; but she does not come in a carriage. She flutters down from the moon.

> A LITTLE fairy comes at night,
>   Her eyes are blue, her hair is brown,
> With silver spots upon her wings,
>   And from the moon she flutters down.

She has a little silver wand,
    And when a good child goes to bed,
She waves her wand from right to left,
    And makes a circle round its head.

And then it dreams of pleasant things—
    Of fountains filled with fairy fish,
And trees that bear delicious fruit,
    And bow their branches at a wish;

Of arbours filled with dainty scents
    From lovely flowers that never fade;
Bright flies that glitter in the sun,
    And glow-worms shining in the shade;

And talking birds with gifted tongues
    For singing songs and telling tales,
And pretty dwarfs to show the way
    Through fairy hills and fairy dales.

But when a bad child goes to bed,
   From left to right she weaves her rings,
And then it dreams all through the night
   Of only ugly horrid things!

Then lions come with glaring eyes,
   And tigers growl—a dreadful noise;
And ogres draw their cruel knives
   To shed the blood of girls and boys.

Then stormy waves rush on to drown,
   And raging flames come scorching round,
Fierce dragons hover in the air,
   And serpents crawl along the ground.

Then wicked children wake and weep,
   And wish the long black gloom away:
But good ones love the dark, and find
   The night as pleasant as the day.

THOMAS HOOD.

EXERCISES

1. What gifts does Queen Mab give to good and to bad children?
2. How does she wave her wand over good children?
3. How over bad?
4. What are in the arbours that good children dream of?
5. What can the fairy birds do?
6. What do the dwarfs do?
7. What are ogres?
8. Where are the dragons seen?
9. Where do the serpents crawl?
10. What do wicked children wish about the night?

LESSON 5

PALMS

ALL children who live in tropical countries are used to seeing palms both in gardens and growing wild. Those who live in temperate countries have often never seen them, and only know them from pictures. This is because very few palms can grow in cold countries except in houses made of glass which are always kept warm.

Some palms have leaves like large feathers, as you will notice if you look at the coconut and gru-gru[*]; others have large fan-shaped leaves, such as the carat. The cabbage palm has a very smooth stem, but that of the gru-gru is very prickly. Some palms make only one tall, straight trunk, like the cabbage palm or palmiste; others make many slender ones, like the black Roseau.[†] Some are climbers, such as the lattan of Tobago. If you visit the Botanic Gardens in your island you will see many different kinds which have been brought from various hot countries.

All palms will not grow under the same conditions. The coconut grows best near sandy beaches; others, such as the carat and timite, are found amidst the moisture, shade, and gloom of the high woods or forests. The date palm grows best in dry countries, its home being near the great

[*] "Supa" in Belize. [†] Bastard or Pimento palm.

African desert known as the Sahara. You will have noticed that gru-gru palms are only found on dry hillsides, and you might look for them in vain in the moist forest. The black Roseau, on the other hand, grows best in swamps, and dies if planted in a dry place.

The most valuable and most widely cultivated of all palms is the coconut. It is found in nearly all tropical countries, and has been grown so long that we do not know from which country it came first. People like to drink the water of the "green nuts," and children are fond of sugar cakes made from the grated meat of the nut mixed with sugar. It has, however, other and more important uses, the chief of which is for coconut oil. The kernel of the coconut, after it has been taken out of the shell and dried in the sun, is known as copra. This is sent abroad, where it is pressed to get out the oil, which has many uses. The husk of the nut is used for a large number of purposes, such as making brushes, mats, and mattresses.

On the west coast of Africa the most common palm is the oil palm, which covers vast areas of the tropical jungle. Soap and candles are largely made from the oil taken from the seeds of this palm. The natives of that country also use them for food. In Northern Africa and the Sahara the date is the common palm. Its fruit is largely used for food. This palm does not grow well in the West Indies, but the dried fruits are sold in the stores, and the tree is grown as a garden palm.

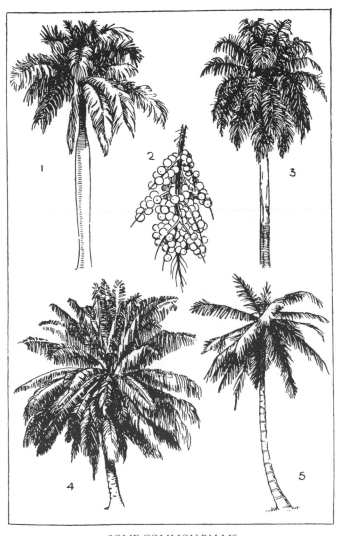

SOME COMMON PALMS

1. Cabbage Palm. 2. Fruit of Gri-gri Palm. 3. Gru-gru Palm.
4. Oil Palm. 5. Coconut Palm.

Many other palms are useful. In Trinidad the leaves of the carat palm are much used for thatching houses, as are also those of the timite.

The scarlet fruits of the gri-gri and the yellowish fruits of the pewa are very good to eat, and are often sold in the market. From the bud of the palmiste we get palm cabbage, which is very delicious.

You see that palms have many uses—many more, in fact, than it is possible to mention here. Some of them, such as the coconut, the oil, and the date palms, are amongst the most useful plants in the world.

Lastly, we must not forget that palms when grown in pots or tins are very pretty, and improve the appearance of our houses.

EXERCISES

1. Write out the names of palms which give us food.
2. In another list give those which are useful in other ways.
3. Put those which are of little use in a third list.
4. Write out these names in a list, and show beside each one where it grows best:—
    date palm.
    gru-gru.
    coconut.
    oil palm.
    carat.
    black Roseau.
5. Make a drawing of the coconut palm.

LESSON 6

ODYSSEUS AND THE CYCLOPS.—I

ONCE upon a time there was a very brave and cunning man named Odysseus. About three thousand years ago, a blind poet of Greece, named Homer, wrote a long poem about Odysseus.

In this poem he tells how Odysseus wandered for ten years, and at last came back to his home in the island of Ithaca. During his wanderings he had many adventures; and I am now going to tell you about his adventures in the land of the Cyclopes, who were one-eyed giants.

These cruel giants lived on a far-off island. They were as tall as trees, and each had one round eye in the middle of his forehead.

They kept sheep and goats, which fed all day in the fields, and were driven home at night to the caves in which the giants lived.

One night Odysseus and his crew came in their ship to the land of those one-eyed giants. They got out of their ship and lay down on the seashore, and slept till morning. Early next day Odysseus and twelve of his crew, taking a skin full of wine and a bag of food with them, went inland until they came to the cave of a Cyclops.

This Cyclops was away from home feeding his sheep, so Odysseus and his sailors went into the cave. There they saw presses filled with cheese,

vessels full of milk covered with cream, and a number of pens with lambs and kids in them.

The sailors begged Odysseus to drive the kids and lambs down to the ship at once. He did not listen to them, but said that he would wait in the cave until the Cyclops came back.

Towards sunset the giant (whose name was Polyphemus) came home, carrying on his shoulder a number of dry sticks and logs of wood, which he threw down with a loud noise.

Odysseus and his crew were astonished to see the huge giant with only one eye, and they were so frightened that they hid themselves in the inner part of the cave, hoping that they would not be seen.

Polyphemus drove his sheep and goats into the cave, and shut up the doorway with a huge stone. Then he milked the ewes and the goats, and lit his fire.

The fire burned so brightly that the giant spied the strangers. "Who are you?" he asked, "and what are you doing here?" Odysseus said that they had been driven to the island by a storm.

The giant did not answer Odysseus, but leapt up, took hold of two of the sailors by their legs, and dashed their heads on the ground. Then he cut them in pieces, and ate them; after which he stretched himself on the floor, and went to sleep.

You may be sure that Odysseus and his men were much afraid. They wept, and prayed to their gods, and looked about for a way of escape; but they could find none.

Odysseus was going to stab the sleeping Polyphemus with his sword, when he remembered that only the giant could roll away the stone from the doorway of the cave. He therefore determined not to kill the giant.

EXERCISES

1. What did the crew beg Odysseus to do?
2. What did Odysseus and his crew hope for?
3. How tall were the Cyclopes?
4. How many eyes had Polyphemus?
5. Where was his eye?
6. How many of the crew went with Odysseus?

Polyphemus and Cyclops

7. What did the rest do?
8. What animals did the Cyclopes keep?
9. Where did they live?
10. What was their food?
11. Who wrote the poem about Odysseus?
12. In this Lesson and the Exercises the words "Cyclops" and "Cyclopes" are both used. Which is used for *one* giant, and which for *more than one?*

LESSON 7

THE BLOOD

EVERY child knows that the red fluid which appears when the skin is cut is named blood. Have you ever wondered what this fluid is made of, and of what use it is to your body?

The blood is really a colourless fluid, in which float many millions of very small bodies—the blood corpuscles or "blood discs." You know that a *disc* is a flat round thing like a coin. Those in the blood are so small, however, that you could only see them with a microscope.

These corpuscles are of two kinds—red and white. The red ones are shaped something like a cent piece slightly hollowed out on both sides. They contain a red substance which gives to the blood its special colour. The white ones are not so numerous as the red ones, but they have a very important work to do.

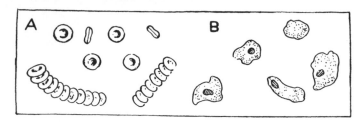

Blood Corpuscles seen through a Microscope.
A, red corpuscles; B, white corpuscles.

The blood is found in every part of the body, and is contained in tubes called blood vessels, in which it is kept moving by the force of the heart's beat. This movement of the blood all through the body is known as the *circulation of the blood.*

The heart is a wonderful organ, constantly at work pumping the blood, and doing this work so quietly that you are aware of it only when you feel it thumping against the left side of your chest after you have been running hard or playing at some game.

Now we will consider how our bodies make use of the blood. They are never quite at rest; some work or growth is always taking place, and so a regular supply of nourishment is necessary. This comes partly from the food we eat and partly from the air we breathe.

The food, after being prepared by the stomach and other organs, reaches the blood as a thin liquid, and is carried in the blood to all parts of the body.

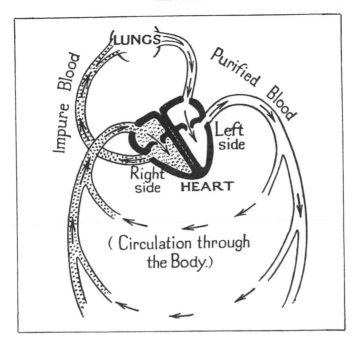

The Circulation of the Blood.

In any engine—and the human body is a marvellous engine—the power to do work must be obtained from fuel or nourishment. In order to change the fuel into power air is necessary. When we breathe we take the air required by our bodies into two organs, named *lungs,* which are made up of a very large number of small chambers somewhat like a sponge. These chambers are surrounded by small blood vessels whose walls are strong enough to keep the blood in, but thin enough to allow the air to pass through and mix with the blood.

The substance which gives their colour to the red corpuscles has a special liking for the chief part of the air—a gas called oxygen. It seizes this gas and carries it to all parts of the body, and it readily gives up to each part the supply of oxygen which is needed to keep it alive.

The heart is divided into a right and left half, with special blood vessels leading to and from the lungs. The blood passes from the right side of the heart to the lungs to obtain its new supply of oxygen, and then returns to the left side of the heart to be sent all over the body.

We now see the reason for the red discs, or corpuscles. They carry and deliver oxygen to the tissues and keep on returning to the lungs for fresh supplies. The white ones, however, have a different duty. They make a sort of medicine that fights the poison made by any germs which get into the blood.

Besides carrying nourishment, the blood takes away and gets rid of waste and useless products which would poison us if allowed to remain in the tissues, and it also helps to keep the heat or temperature of our bodies at a proper level.

EXERCISES

1. Fill in the blanks:—

There are more _____ corpuscles then _____ ones.

Food is taken to all parts of the body by the _____ in the form of a _____.

The red discs hold oxygen very lightly, and so _____ give it up.

The heart is really a strong —— which sends the
—— all through the ——.

2. What is the circulation of the blood?
3. The blood may be said to be like both the grocer's van and the sanitary cart. Why?
4. In what ways is the body like an engine?
5. Where can you feel the *pumping* of the blood as well as on the left side of your chest?

LESSON 8

THE FISHES IN OUR WATERS.—I

SEA FISHES

THE fishes that inhabit our seas are most important, as they provide a large supply of wholesome food. The biggest monsters in the world live in the sea; some of these, such as whales and porpoises, are not true fishes, but are really mammals.

There are more than two hundred kinds of salt-water fishes found in the seas round the West Indies. The most important are those that are brought to the market to be sold for food—namely, the king-fish, mackerel, snapper or red-fish, grouper, mullet, cavalli or carangue, dolphin, and bonito. There are many other kinds which are eatable, but these are the best known.

A great many fishes are unfit for food or not pleasant to the taste, and some are poisonous. Fortunately the fishes that are the most abundant

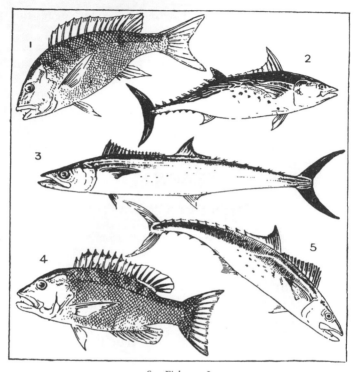

Sea Fishes.—I.
1. Mutton fish. 2. Bonito. 3. King-fish 4. Gray Snapper.
5. Spanish Mackerel.
(*From Drawings by Mr. P. L. Guppy.*)

are those that we like best, such as king-fish, mackerel, and snapper. The *Coryphæna* dolphin and bonito are also plentiful in some parts.

The tarpon or "cuffum" is much sought after by anglers who fish for sport, but it is not much desired as food. It has very large scales.

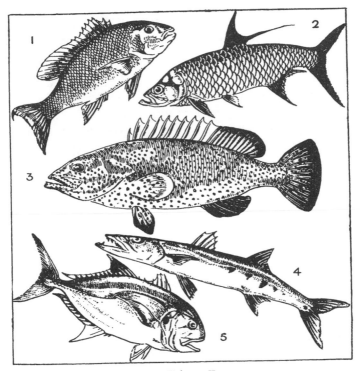

Sea Fishes.—II.
1. Red-fish. 2. Tarpon. 3. Grouper. 4. Barracouta. 5. Cavalli.
(*From Drawings by Mr. P. L. Guppy.*)

There are various ways of catching fish, such as trolling, banking, and torchlight fishing, and hand-nets, seines, and fish-traps are the means in most common use.

The hand-nets are useful for catching sardines and small fry to be used as bait when trolling.

Seines are long nets used to surround the fish that come into the bays near the shore, such as king-fish, mackerel, bonito, and cavalli.

Mackerel and king-fish are caught by trolling as well as by seines, but some fishes, like the *Coryphæna* dolphin, can be caught by trolling only, as they do not come near enough to the shore to be taken in seines.

Red-fish and snappers are fished for with very long lines to which weights are attached; several hooks baited with fish are placed above the weights. Large snappers and groupers are caught by this means at great depths, where they go to feed on various creatures, such as crabs, lobsters, and shrimps, that live among the rocky "banks" at the bottom of the sea. This method of fishing is called "banking."

Fish-traps are used mostly among the rocks and reefs. They are usually called "fish-pots," and everyone has seen these clever traps, into which the fish can find their way, but from which they cannot escape. Many wonderful and beautiful fishes are caught in such traps. Some of these are "parrot-fish," "grunts," and chubs. Many of those caught in this way are not much valued as food, though some are edible.

Torchlight-fishing is a method by which small fish are obtained for bait. The fish are attracted by the flare of a torch on a dark night. This method is also used for catching crayfish, crabs, and other shell-fish.

Two of the monsters of the deep which are dangerous to man, and will attack him in the water, are the shark and the barracouta. The latter is famous for its terrible teeth, of which the foremost ones in each jaw fit into grooves in the other jaw. The fish grows to over eight feet in length.

The shark has to turn over on its side when it seizes anything which is above it in the water, as its mouth is so far under the lower part of its head. It can raise its teeth upright or let them lie at rest.

There are also "porcupine" fish all bristling with spines, "sea-horses," "cow-fish" with horns, "butterfly" fish, swell-toads, and others too numerous to mention.

Note for Teacher.—The *Coryphæna dolphin* should not be confused with the *Delphinus dolphin*, from which it differs entirely. The former is a gorgeously coloured fish, but the latter is a dark-hued, porpoise-like creature which is compelled to rise to the surface of the water to breathe. It is a mammal. Explain the difference to the pupils.

EXERCISES

1. There are two words in this lesson which mean "fit to eat." What are they?
2. Make from this lesson a list of the fishes you have eaten, and another list of those you have not eaten.
3. In what ways are fish caught? Give the names of those which are caught in each of these different ways.
4. Some fishes attack man. Some are dangerous in other ways. Name them.

LESSON 9

WEST INDIAN POEMS

The Bahamas

WHERE the flaming poin-
ciana* and the ever-waving
palm
And the low palmetto
scrub are broadly cast,
O'er the sunny islands
smiling still in tempest
and in calm
Lives the record of a
strange and storied past.

Bahamian Ballads and Rhymes.

Guyana: El Dorado

The City of Gold

HAVE you read of the city of
gold,
Which the myths of the past
enfold?
Over the seas the searchers
came,
And sought for the shining
towers in vain.
A few returned; but the rest
were slain;
Alas, for the dream of old!

* Flamboyante.

The mythical city of gold
Glittered with wealth untold
In the midst of a lake of sapphire blue;
The shores of the lake were golden, too;
And around the lake dense forests grew
That baffled the searchers bold.

Long has the tale been told;
Still does its glamour hold;
But, till the mists of Time unfold,
No mortal eyes will e'er behold
The city with the streets of gold—
It lies where the stars are rolled.

> From *History of the West Indies,*
> by ALLISTER MACMILLAN.
> (*By permission.*)

JAMAICA

THE great Creator, shaping sun and star,
　Heard an Archangel speaking thus: "I
　　dreamed
I saw another Paradise, afar;
　And all about it sapphire waters gleamed."
The Maker smiled. At His
　　divine behest
The Angel's dream like
　　some blush rose uncurled,
To bloom for ever on the
　　warm sea's breast,
The beautiful Jamaica of
　　the world.

ELLA WHEELER WILCOX.

Trinidad: Iëre

Land of the Humming Bird

THOSE who eat the *cascadura* will, the native legend says,
Wheresoever they may wander, end in Trinidad their days.
And this lovely fragrant island, with its forest hills sublime,
Well might be the smiling Eden pictured in the Book divine.

Cocoa woods with scarlet glory of the stately Immortelles,
Waterfalls and fertile valleys, precipices, fairy dells,
Rills and rivers, green savannahs, fruits and flowers and odours rich,
Waving sugar cane plantations and the wondrous lake of pitch.

Oh! the Bocas at the daybreak—how can one
　　describe that scene!
Or the little emerald islands with the sapphire
　　sea between!
Matchless country of Iëre, fairer none could ever
　　wish.
Can you wonder at the legend of the *cascadura*
　　fish?

From *History of the West Indies*,
by ALLISTER MACMILLAN.
(*By permission.*)

EXERCISES

1. A sapphire is a jewel. What is its colour? What jewels
    have the following colours: (i.) red, (ii.) green,
    (iii.) colourless, but shining brilliantly when cut?
2. Try to make a verse about your own country. Do
    you know of any poem in which your country is
    mentioned?
3. Give other words for
      the Book Divine   baffled   legend
      the Great Creator   enfold   fragrant
      poinciana   behest   myths
4. Two lakes are mentioned in these poems. In what ways
    do they differ?
5. Why did the Archangel say "*another* Paradise"? What
    was the first?
6. What incident do you know of in the "record of a
    strange and storied past" of the Bahamas? Where did
    you learn of it?
7. What do you think was the origin of the story of El
    Dorado? Has any gold been found in Guyana?

LESSON 10

ODYSSEUS AND THE CYCLOPS.—II

ALL night long the Greeks lay awake in great fear, waiting for the dawn. When the sun's first beams shone into the cave Polyphemus got up, lit his fire, and milked his goats. Then he seized two more of the sailors, and ate them for breakfast.

After breakfast he moved away the great door-stone, and drove his sheep and goats out of the cave. Then he put the stone back in its place, and drove his flocks towards the hills, leaving Odysseus and his men to wonder which of them would be eaten next.

While Polyphemus was away, Odysseus was trying to think of a way to escape. At last he thought of a very clever way, and we shall soon see what it was.

By the side of a sheep-pen he saw the giant's great wooden club, as big as the mast of a ship. From this great club Odysseus cut a stake, and sharpened it to a point. Then he hardened the point in the fire, and hid the stake.

In the evening Polyphemus came home, and when he had milked his goats and lighted his fire he seized two more of the sailors, and killed and ate them for his supper.

Then Odysseus offered him some of the wine that he had brought from the ship, and the giant drank it off, and asked for more. He liked the wine so much that he said to Odysseus, "What is your name? I wish to give you a reward."

Then Odysseus said, "My name is Nobody."

"Well, Nobody," said the giant, "this shall be your reward: I will eat you the last of all."

Then Polyphemus drank the rest of the wine, and soon fell into a drunken sleep. He lay on the floor, with his face upturned; and while he slept Odysseus heated the sharpened end of the stake in the fire.

Then, when all was ready, he and his friends thrust the stake into the giant's one eye. The giant awoke, and with a loud roar pulled out the stake.

Roaring with pain, he rushed round and round the cave, trying to catch Odysseus and his men. But as the giant was now blind, they were easily able to keep out of his way.

The giant was still roaring with pain, and soon wakened his neighbours, who gathered round the cave, and cried "Who is killing you?"

"*Nobody* is killing me!" he cried. "*Nobody* is killing me!"

"If nobody is killing you," they said, "why do you make this great hubbub?"

"*Nobody* is killing me!" he cried again and again.

Thinking that he was mad, the giants left him, and went off to their own homes. Odysseus laughed to think how he had tricked them.

But Odysseus and his friends were not out of danger yet. Next morning when Polyphemus rolled away the stone, he sat in the doorway with his arms stretched out, hoping to catch them if they tried to go out with the sheep.

EXERCISES

1. Were Odysseus and his crew able to roll away the door-stone?
2. How large was the Cyclops's club?
3. Which of the Greeks was Polyphemus going to eat last?
4. Why was he going to eat Odysseus last?
5. Why did Odysseus say that his name was "Nobody"?
6. How many of the Greeks did Polyphemus eat?
7. Why did he not eat more?

LESSON 11

VOLCANOES

SOME people call volcanoes "burning mountains," but that is not a good name for them. They are not all mountains, and they do not burn.

Section of Volcano.

A volcano is usually a mountain or a hill with a great hole like a chimney running deep down into the earth. This opening often sends out clouds of steam, which many people

The Crater of a Volcano during an Eruption.

call smoke, because it is dark with dust and stones. The mouth of the opening or vent is called the *crater* of the volcano.

If we could look into this opening it would give us a peep into the inside of this globe on which we live; we should see that under the cool and solid ground the earth is very hot. This is almost the only thing we know about the inside of the earth.

The hardest rock is melted there as if it were in a furnace; and this molten rock, called *lava,*

Hot Spring.

often flows out of the crater of a volcano and pours down the hillside. When it cools, it forms a hard black rock.

The lava and the stones from the crater build up a mound or hill round it; and so a mountain is made by the action of the heat inside the earth.

In many places hot water and steam come out of holes in the ground. A hot spring, or *geyser*, as it is often called, is really a kind of volcano.

There are many hills and mountains in the West Indies which were at one time volcanoes. They are now *extinct,* as we say; their vents are closed up and their fires seem to have gone out. In 1902, however, two of them were active, but they are now peacefully asleep again. They were Mont Pelé in Martinique and the Soufrière in St. Vincent.

On May 7th of that year the Soufrière suddenly burst into violent eruption after being quiet for ninety years. The roar, as of thunder,

St. Pierre, Martinique, before the Eruption.

was heard as far as Barbados, one hundred miles away, as well as in Grenada, Trinidad, and St. Lucia. Ashes were carried by the wind even to Barbados, where they fell.

The following day, after many inward rumblings and other signs of action, a huge mass of fiery material burst from the side of Mont Pelé and rushed down upon the town of St. Pierre, which nestled in a valley at its foot. Masses of molten lava and ashes covered all the buildings, and fully 40,000 people lost their lives.

Even the ships in the harbour were destroyed by the fiery mass, which swept like a river over the town and pushed the very waters of the sea before it. It is said that only one man, a prisoner in his cell, was saved, and not a building escaped in the terrible catastrophe. The ruins may still be seen where once stood one of the prettiest towns in the West Indies.

Exercises

1. Give the date of the eruption of Mont Pelé.
2. What other words do you know that have a meaning somewhat like "catastrophe"?
3. What do we know about the inside of the earth? How do we know it?
4. How is a mountain made by the action of the heat inside the earth?
5. Fill in the blanks:—

> The lumps of hard black rock were once ——, and were called ——.
>
> This volcano was once ——, but is now ——.
>
> Let us climb it and look into the ——.
>
> Hot springs, or ——, are really ——.
>
> The Barbadians called the —— "May Dust" when they fell on their ——.

St. Pierre after the Eruption.

LESSON 12

THE MUSIC OF WORDS

I

You already know a large number of words. In years to come, when you read many books, you will learn many more words. Think of the words which you already know. Some of them are sweet and beautiful, and fall off the tongue smoothly. Others are hard and rough, and are not easy to say.

Read the following lines:—

> "Home they brought her warrior dead;
>   She nor swooned nor uttered cry;
>   All her maidens watching, said,
>   'She must weep, or she will die.'"

I think you will say that the words of this little verse are very sweet, and that they are put together in such a way that they seem to sing to us.

Some men and women are very skilful in choosing sweet words and putting them together so as to please our ears and make us feel and think. If their work is very good, and if they make us feel deeply, or think of noble things, we call them poets, and we say that they write poetry. The minstrels of old were not only poets, but makers of music as well.

Read the little verse again. If you were telling a friend about the poor lady, you would not speak as the poet does. You would perhaps say, "Her husband was a soldier, and they brought him home dead. When she saw his body, she neither fainted nor cried. The maids who were watching her said, 'We must do something to make her weep, or she will die.'"

Now, when you read these words, you will perhaps say, "Oh, this is just everyday talk. There is neither beauty nor music in it. I could not make up the verse, but I could say that." Quite right. When we put words together in an everyday, straightforward way, we are speaking or writing what is called *prose,* and prose is very different from poetry.

I once read of a Frenchman who was ignorant, but wished to learn. He went to a teacher, and one of the first things he learned was that everyday talk is called prose. The Frenchman was delighted. "How clever I am!" he said. "All my life I have been talking prose without knowing it!"

Most of the books which people now read are written in prose, but the oldest books of all were written in poetry. The story of Odysseus was told in poetry.

You can easily understand why poetry came before prose. The minstrels wished to stir men's minds and hearts, so they chose their words with great care. As they sang their stories to the harp,

"SONS OF THE BRAVE" (THE BOYS OF THE DUKE
OF YORK'S SCHOOL.)
(*From the painting by Phil Morris A.R.A.*)

the words had to be put together in such a way that they would run smoothly and go with the music. It is also easier to remember the words of poetry than of prose.

II

When you sing a song in school your teacher beats time for you. You follow the beat, and thus you all keep together and put the stress on the right notes. A song must be sung both in time and in tune if it is to give pleasure.

When soldiers march, the band goes before them playing a tune, and the drum-major swings his staff in order that the bandsmen may keep time. You can see a drum-major in the picture on page 53.

Now we can also beat time to poetry—

A-róund | the fire | one wín- | try níght, |
    The fár- | mer's ró- | sy chíl- | dren sát; |
The fág- | ot lént | its blá- | zing líght, |
    And jókes | went róund | and cáre- | less chát. |

You see that I have drawn upright lines so as to break each line of the verse into four parts. All that is printed between any two of these upright lines we will call a *foot*.

In the verse which you have just read there are two beats in each foot, an up beat and a down beat. The up beat is the weak beat, the down beat is the strong beat. We put stress on that word or part of a word which goes with the down beat. In the verse the strong or down beat is marked by an accent (´).

You must not expect every verse to be built up in this way. If all verses had the strong beats in the same place we should soon tire of them. Just as a man can make carpets of different patterns by weaving the threads differently, so a poet can make verses of different patterns by arranging the strong and weak beats differently.

Here is a verse of a different pattern from that which you have just read—

Sée the | kít-ten | ón the | wáll,

Spórt-ing | with the | léaves that | fáll—

With-ered | léaves, one, | twó, and | thrée,

Fáll-ing | fróm the | él-der | trée,

Through the | cálm and | fróst-y | áir

Óf the | mórn-ing, | bright and | fair.

Now look carefully at the verse about the farmer's rosy children. Notice the last word in the first line and the last word in the third line—*night, light.* These words have almost the same sound. Four out of the five letters which make up the words are the same; only the first letter is different. Words which have much the same sound are said to rhyme. The words *night, bright, sight, right,* and so on, all rhyme.

In much of our poetry we find rhymes. Sometimes each pair of lines ends with a rhyme, as in the verse about the kitten. Sometimes every other line ends with a rhyme, as in the verse about the farmer's children. Most people like rhymes, because they please the ear and seem to give more music to the verse.

You must not suppose that there is no poetry without rhymes. Some of the best poetry ever written has no rhymes at all. Rhyme is like the frill of a frock—it sets off the frock; but many very beautiful frocks have no frills at all.

EXERCISE

When you read the poetry in this book, try to find out how many feet each line has, and where the strong beat comes in each foot. You will soon learn to do this for yourself, and it will help you to enjoy the poetry better.

LESSON 13

SOME USEFUL PLANTS

HAVE you ever thought how many plants there are which you make use of every day? Some of them form your chief articles of food.

People in other countries would be surprised to see the strange uses to which we put some of our plants. We scrub our clothes with a corn cob and our houses with a coconut husk. Some people are very clever in making bush teas for all kinds of complaints. When we are caught in the rain a banana leaf makes a splendid umbrella. These leaves are also largely used by bakers for covering their bread. In place of string we can use lianes, langue bœuf,* or other fibres. Soap seeds are sometimes used for washing instead of soap. We wrap our meat in papaw leaves to make it tender. Calabashes make useful water-carriers and bowls. Bamboos and palm leaves are made into brooms.

Calabash.

Besides all these, there are numerous other uses for our plants. Boys often use a coconut leaf stalk for a cricket bat, or a leaf sheath for a toboggan on a dry slope.

We will think now of a few of the commoner plants which are used for food. There is the

Ground Nuts.

ground nut or pistache, which is often cooked and sold under the name of salt nuts. The plant has a peculiar habit of burying its seed-pods in the ground. These must be dug up with a fork.

A brightly coloured and favourite drink is made from the covering of the seed-pods of the sorrel. They ripen about Christmas time.

* "Henequén" in Belize.

Huge pumpkins and water-melons are very plentiful at certain seasons. Ochroes are grown

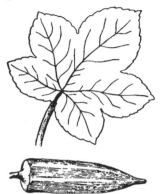

throughout the year. There are several kinds, all being slimy when cooked. They are often used for mixing with corn-meal coo-coo.

We have plenty of good peas and beans, the best known of which are black-eye peas and pigeon peas. Lesser known kinds are salad beans, red

Ochro Leaf and Fruit.

beans, black beans, and bodi. Black peas are often planted on rice lands soon after the rice crop is reaped. They mature very quickly, and because of this are sometimes called "six weeks bean." Pigeon peas are grown in almost every garden.

Many salads grow well. Lettuce, cucumbers, and water-cress are the most common. In the dry hills, carrots, chives, and thyme are grown.

Cucumber.

Tomatoes are much used in West Indian cookery. They can be bought throughout the year, though in the wet season only a small kind can be grown except in the driest places.

Peppers of many kinds and colours are common, such as bird pepper, coffee pepper, and cherry pepper. Some of the larger kinds have a very hot flavour. Their chief use is in cooking and for making pepper sauce.

Tomato.

There are many other kinds of useful food plants. Cabbage is now commonly grown. The

Peppers.

purple melongene (boulanger or egg plant) is very plentiful. There are also many spice plants, such as clove, cinnamon, nutmeg, and vanilla.

Europeans who come to live here find that they can get most of the

Melongene.

vegetables to which they have been accustomed at home, and also many which they have never seen before.

Exercises

1. Arrange the plants named in this lesson in three columns—
   - (i.) Those useful for food.
   - (ii.) Those useful for other purposes only.
   - (iii.) Those useful for both food and other purposes.
2. What is the "six weeks bean"? Why is it so called?
3. How many spices are mentioned in this lesson? What are they?
4. How do ground nuts get into the ground?
5. Fill in the blanks:—

Singular	Plural
tomato	——
——	mangoes
ochro	——
——	eddoes

LESSON 14

THE FISHES IN OUR WATERS.—II

Fresh-water Fishes

IN Lesson 8 you have read of the fishes which live in our seas. Fresh-water fishes are also of great importance, especially in Guyana, Belize and the larger West Indian islands. There are over forty kinds in Trinidad alone, and very many more in other islands and on the Main.

Some fresh-water fishes really belong to the sea, but go a long way up the rivers. One of these is the broche or snook, which is sometimes

20 pounds in weight. It can even be bred in fresh-water pools.

Fishes are not only of value as food, but many species are useful as mosquito destroyers, and others as scavengers.

"Millions" or "belly-fish" are well known throughout the West Indies. You will see some of them in the picture, where they are shown in their true size. The male is the smaller, and it often has a round black spot on each side, and also brightly-coloured spots, green or red or blue.

The great value of this little fish, which multiplies so rapidly, is that it feeds on the eggs and larvæ of the mosquito. You have learned that this insect lays its eggs and spends its early life in water, and so "millions" are friends of mankind in helping to destroy this pest. They have been introduced into many countries in the hope that they will thus check malaria.

The guabin or dormeuse is much liked by some people, but it is very bony. It is also a useful mosquito destroyer, and is found in many islands and on the Main. It inhabits pools of water on the Pitch Lake in Trinidad, as also does the "small guabin," a fish closely related to the "millions." This fish is another enemy of the mosquito.

There are seven different kinds of fish known as sardines, the most common being the pink-finned sardine. The cutlass-fish is sometimes caught in swamps.

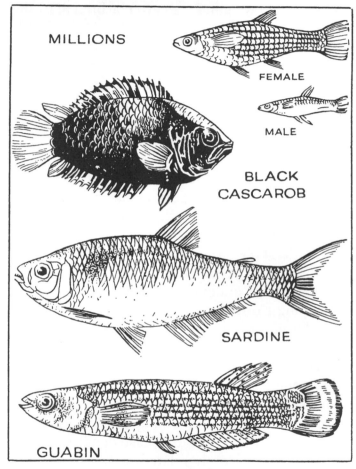

MILLIONS

FEMALE

MALE

BLACK
CASCAROB

SARDINE

GUABIN

Fresh-water Fishes.
(*From Drawings by Mr. P. L. Guppy.*)

The king or black cascarob will eat almost
anything. It dwells in muddy rivers and ponds,
and has the wonderful habit of changing its
colour when excited. The small cascarob is an

elegant little fish, which tries to defend its young when they are attacked.

The cascadura or "armoured hassar" is marketed in the dry season, and is considered by many people a great delicacy. This fish has no scales, but is covered with armour in the form of bony plates. It lives for some time after being taken out of the water, it grunts when handled, and it defends its nests. It is mentioned in the poems on pages 42 and 125.

Eels live in rivers under rocks or buried in mud. In Guyana there is a large electric eel which gives a powerful electric shock when touched.

The arapaima, a large bony fish, lives in the rivers of Guyana. It is said to be the biggest fish found in fresh water. Sometimes it weighs more than 250 pounds.

On the Main there is also the caribe or perai, a savage little fish with triangular teeth. It will attack any small animal that is wounded, and tear it to pieces.

EXERCISES

1. Why do you think those little fishes are called "millions"?
2. Is the snook a sea fish or a river fish?
3. Draw the fishes shown on page 62.
4. Write out all the names of the fishes given in this lesson. Which of them have you seen?
5. Do you know any other fresh-water fishes not named? If so, what are they?

LESSON 15

ODYSSEUS AND THE CYCLOPS.—III
(*See Frontispiece.*)

ODYSSEUS was quite as cunning as the giant. After much thought he found a way for himself and his friends to escape.

He took a number of osiers,[*] of which Polyphemus's bed was made, and with them tied the huge rams together in threes. Underneath the middle ram of each three he tied one of his men.

Then he himself twisted his hands and feet into the thick wool of the best ram of the flock, and lying curled up under it, he waited for the coming of the dawn.

When the sun rose, the sheep bleated loudly, and went out to feed. Polyphemus, still in great pain, felt along their backs as they passed.

He wished to make quite sure that Odysseus and his men were not on the backs of the sheep or between them. He little thought that they were tied underneath the rams.

The last to come out was the large and beautiful ram which carried Odysseus. As soon as he had passed the giant, Odysseus loosed himself from under the ram, and set his friends free.

Rapidly the Greeks drove many of the sheep to the ship, and put them aboard. Then they

---

[*] *Osiers* are young twigs of the willow tree, and are used for making baskets.

ESCAPE OF ODYSSEUS AND HIS MEN.

took their oars and rowed the vessel out a little distance from the land.

Before setting sail, Odysseus shouted to the giant, and told him that the gods had punished him for his wicked deeds.

This made the giant very angry. He broke off the top of a high hill, and threw it at the ship. It fell in front of the ship, and raised a great wave, which drove the vessel back on the shore.

Then Odysseus seized a long pole, and thrust the ship off the land. The men worked at the oars with all their strength, and soon the ship was out of danger.

Once more Odysseus shouted to the giant: "If any man asks who put out your eye, tell him that it was Odysseus."

When Polyphemus heard this, he begged Odysseus to come on shore again, that he might show him kindness, and treat him well.

But Odysseus only laughed. Then the angry giant threw another huge rock at the ship. It fell close to the rudder, and only helped to move the vessel on more quickly.

The Greeks rowed hard, and their ship bounded over the sparkling waves. Soon the island of the Cyclopes faded away in the distance, and at last was lost sight of below the horizon.

You can read more of the adventures of Odysseus and his men in a little book called *Stories from the Odyssey.*

Exercises

1. With what did Odysseus tie his men to the rams?
2. Why did Polyphemus feel the rams as they went out?
3. Why did he not find Odysseus and his men?
4. Which ram went out last?
5. What did the Greeks do when they were free?
6. What did Odysseus do before setting sail?
7. What did the giant do?
8. How did Odysseus get the ship off the shore?
9. What was the last thing Odysseus said to the giant?
10. What did Polyphemus beg of Odysseus?
11. What did Odysseus do then?
12. Why did the Greeks lose sight of the island of the Cyclopes?

LESSON 16

PLANTS AND THEIR HOMES

HAVE you ever studied plants in their homes, and noticed the different conditions under which they grow? Let us pay a short visit to some of them together.

After leaving the school we pass grasses of various kinds on the dry roadside. Amongst these is the sensitive plant or shame

Sensitive Plant.

bush, which closes its leaves at the slightest touch.

Castor-oil Plant.

Next we see the castor-oil plant with its fan-shaped leaves, then a hedge of wild coffee bushes, and now a red Ixora. We soon come to a slowly-running stream of water. On the surface float the leaves of water-lilies, the roots of which are firmly fastened in the mud. We cannot see any flowers on this particular kind, as they only open at night. They are then white, and very sweetly scented.

Walking a little way up the stream we reach wooded country. Here the undergrowth is composed of all kinds of ferns, small palms, and low bush. Towering overhead are large palms

Water-lilies.

and giant timber trees, such as the cedar, which is much used for house-building. "Wild pines" and orchids grow thickly on their branches. If we had time to climb the mountain in the distance we should find the forest more dense. Tree ferns grow there in large numbers.

A little farther on we come to a place where the high woods have been felled for timber and charcoal burning. Here low bush has begun to grow, and we find guava bush, razor and other large grasses, black sage, and many plants the names of which we do not know.

Wild Pine.

That plant with orange-coloured thread-like branches smothering some of the low bush is the love vine, and the red-and-black seeds of that other tiny little vine are a kind of jumbie bead.

We next come to open grass land, on which the only large plants are certain kinds of palms, such as the moriche and the cocorite. These open tracts of land are known as natural savannahs. They are never entirely covered with bush. All kinds of tiny orchids, bladder-worts, and sundews are growing among the grass.

In the far distance we see the sea; but what is that broad green belt which prevents us from reaching the water's edge? It is a forest of mangrove trees. As we get closer we see that the land is swampy and that the trunks of the mangroves are raised on stilt-like roots. In those parts of the swamp where there is not quite so much water we find dense clumps of the black Roseau palm and a large fern.

Farther along the coast there is no swamp. Here we find the manchineel growing quite close to where the sea reaches at high tide. Its green, roundish fruits are lying all along the shore.

Turk's Cap Cactus.

We must take care not to blister our skin with the milky juice. The trees hung with bunches of purple fruits are seaside grapes. On the more exposed beaches the trees are often clipped by the wind into a neat hedge. Those vines running along the sand are a kind of sword bean and a morning glory.

If we had time I should like to take you to the drier parts of the island. There we should find several kinds of cactus growing among the rocks. They all have fleshy stems, some tall and straight, others short and rounded like the Turk's cap cactus. Some, as the rachet, have flat stems. Most of them have very strong spines and no leaves. Those lovely white flowers are virgin orchids, and the plants with fleshy, spear-shaped leaves are the langue-bœuf, from the fibres of which rope is made.

"Scotch Attorney."

The trees growing in these dry places are usually small. Hanging from their branches we find mistletoe and long streamers of "old man's beard." The large roots swinging in the breeze are those of the "wild fig," or "Scotch Attorney." It has started to grow in the fork of a fiddle-wood tree, and will soon surround it with its roots. The wild fig often kills good trees in this way.

EXERCISE

Arrange all the plants named in this lesson as follows:—

Name of plant.	Where found.
Sensitive plant.	Roadsides.
Wild coffee.	Hedges.
....	....
....	....
....	....
etc.	etc.

"THE CREEPING TIDE CAME UP ALONG THE SAND."

LESSON 17

THE SANDS O' DEE

Introduction.—The Dee is a river in the west of England, which has a wide sandy estuary. Mary's father had a farm on the shore of this estuary, and his cattle grazed on an island in it. When the tide was low they could walk over the sand to the island, but at high water the sand was covered.

One stormy evening Mary's mother told her to go and call the cattle home. She went across the sand, but the west wind blew strongly, and the tide rose very rapidly. It also blew in a mist from the sea. Mary lost her way, and was drowned.

The fishermen had put stakes in the bed of the Dee to which they tied their nets. Next morning they saw something bright and shining among the stakes. They thought it was a fish or seaweed, but at last they saw that it was Mary's bright golden hair. They went in a boat and brought her body ashore, and she was buried in a churchyard near.

The fishermen still imagine that on stormy nights they can hear Mary calling the cattle home.

"O MARY, go and call the cattle home,
    And call the cattle home,
    And call the cattle home,
  Across the sands o' Dee!"
The western wind was wild and dank with foam,
    And all alone went she.
  The creeping tide came up along the sand,
    And o'er and o'er the sand,
    And round and round the sand.
  As far as eye could see;

The rolling mist came down and hid the land–
    And never home came she.

"Oh, is it weed, or fish, or floating hair—
    A tress of golden hair,
    A drownèd maiden's hair,
  Above the nets at sea?"
Was never salmon yet that shone so fair
    Among the stakes on Dee.

They brought her in across the rolling foam,
    The cruel, crawling foam,
    The cruel, hungry foam,
  To her grave beside the sea.
But still the boatmen hear her call the cattle home
    Across the sands o' Dee.

CHARLES KINGSLEY.

EXERCISES

1. Where did Mary live?
2. Where is the Dee?
3. What in the poem shows on which side of England the Dee is?
4. Which line shows that the night was stormy?
5. Why did Mary lose her way?
6. What did the fishermen see in their nets?
7. What did they think it was?
8. What was it really?
9. Why is the foam called *cruel*?
10. Why is it called *hungry*?
11. Where did they bury Mary?
12. What do the fishermen still imagine?
13. What do you notice about the first three lines and about the fourth and sixth lines in all the stanzas?

LESSON 18

DISEASE—GERMS—PARASITES

DISEASE or sickness means the absence of that feeling of ease and comfort which we call good health.

There are many different kinds of diseases, and only a few of us are fortunate enough to escape being ill at some time. Most diseases give pain and make us feel ill, and it is not strange that we should wish to know why our bodies get out of order.

Doctors have discovered that many diseases are caused by very small living bodies called germs and parasites. These are so minute that they can only be seen through a microscope. Hundreds of them could pass at the same time through a hole made by a fine needle in a piece of paper.

They can only come from a person suffering from disease, and may get into our bodies in many ways. We may breathe them in when a sick person coughs or sneezes in our faces; we may swallow them in the water we drink or the food we eat; they may reach us if we handle something which has been used by a sick person, such as a handkerchief, a towel, a spoon, or a pencil; or they may be carried by insects such as mosquitoes and flies.

Germs act like seeds of plants, and are often called the seeds of diseases. They feed upon the body of the person whom they enter, by killing and eating the living flesh near them.

They multiply very rapidly. In some cases each one divides into two in about half an hour. This little drawing will show you that if even one germ got into your body at 12 noon, by 1.30 p.m. there would be eight. Now calculate how many there would be by midnight, and you will see

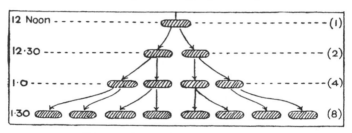

Diagram showing how Germs multiply.

what an enormous quantity would grow from this one in twelve hours. Others increase by producing eggs very quickly.

We may not feel sick for several days after the germs have entered our bodies. During this time they are growing and passing into the blood and putting out poison. When sufficient poison has been produced we begin to feel ill, and the disease appears.

Our bodies are able, fortunately, to make a fight against the germs. As soon as the germs enter our bodies, an army of defence is called up, consisting of the white blood corpuscles and other forces, and a fight begins.

If there is a large number of germs, or if our bodies are weak and badly fed, the germs take the upper hand, and we get the disease; but if our bodies are strong and clean, or the germs are few, the body gets the better of the fight, the germs are killed, and we do not have the disease, or have only a mild attack of it.

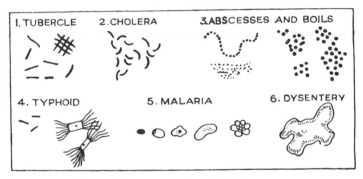

Disease Germs as seen through a Microscope.

We do not know when germs may attack us. We should always be prepared to put up a strong fight, and we can only do this by keeping our bodies clean and healthy.

As germs feed on anything which has had life, we may find them in all refuse, such as dead plants or animals or any of the things that living beings, including ourselves, pass out of their bodies. All these things should, therefore, be destroyed or removed from our houses, so that germs may not increase and lie in wait for a chance to enter our bodies and cause disease.

EXERCISES

1. Parasites are living creatures that live on other living creatures. Some of those which we can see are jiggers, ticks, and fleas. Name any more you know.
2. Those described in this lesson are too small to be seen with the naked eye. How can they be seen? In what ways do they enter the body?
3. What do germs and parasites do in our bodies?
4. How are germs killed?
5. If we want to be healthy we should be clean in every way. Why?

LESSON 19

A HINDU WEDDING

HINDU weddings are celebrated with great pomp in the islands of the West Indies and in Guyana.

After the engagement ceremony, the young people will not see each other until the day of the wedding. The time of marriage is fixed by the pundit, who does this by consulting his books, which tell about the stars and planets that are said to govern the lives of people.

East Indians are very fond of music, and they generally employ musicians and dancers to entertain their guests. Their favourite play,

A Hindu Wedding

Indar Sabha, is often acted on such occasions. On the night of the wedding, and several nights before that, the women are invited to the homes of the bride and bridegroom to sing their songs of love and praise.

Hindu weddings take place during the night. The bridegroom and his friends set out for the bride's house, and her father and the priest, together with her friends, go out to welcome them. As they arrive, the bride's mother goes out with her women-folk to greet them and to go through the welcome ceremony. Immediately after this the bride's father goes through another ceremony with the bridegroom. Many other ceremonies have to be performed which cannot be fully described here.

The bride usually wears a red sari, and at the time of marriage she is brought to the tent which has been erected near her parents' home and is seated on the right-hand side of the bridegroom. East Indians are very coy, and the women hide their faces from men; and so, when the bride is brought to the tent to go through the marriage ceremony, her face is covered with a veil.

The pundit now causes the bride and bridegroom to make sacred vows, promising to be faithful and loving to each other as long as they live. The sacred knot is then tied. The tying of this knot to the sash of the bridegroom and the veil of the bride is a sign that they are joined together for life. In it are a sacred weed, nutmeg, rice, flowers, betel-nut, and money.

The bridegroom then gets a glimpse of his wife. Under a purdah he removes the veil from her head, and as quickly as he can puts the sendoor in the parting in the middle of her hair. The purdah is then lifted and the marriage is complete, and the pundit pronounces them man and wife.

The presents which the bride gets from her relatives and friends are costly and numerous. They consist chiefly of gold and silver jewels, money and precious stones. The bridegroom also receives handsome presents, such as gold coins, bronze ware, and generally a fine milch cow and a piece of land.

East Indians are a very social people. At weddings they invite all their relatives from far and near, and all the people of the town or village where they live. It is a time of merriment and feasting. All who are present, both rich and poor, are fed and well treated.

NOTES

Pundit, a priest.
Purdah, a cloth screen.
Sendoor, a red powder, usually called vermilion.

EXERCISES

1. A wedding is a ceremony. What other ceremonies do you know of?
2. Why do East Indians have musicians at their weddings?
3. What is meant by "the sacred knot"?
4. Write out all the words in the lesson which mean people (either one or more persons).
5. What is a "milch cow"?
6. Fill in the blanks:—

> Some people are said to be born under lucky _____ .
>
> East Indians _____ their friends at their weddings.
>
> The women of many Eastern _____ cover their faces.
>
> The names of _____ metals are given in this lesson.
>
> After the _____ is _____ they are married.

LESSON 20

"TROUBLE MADE THE MONKEY EAT PEPPER"—(CREOLE PROVERB)

A CREOLE FOLK-TALE

ONCE upon a time there was an old woman who lived on the Main, in a very out-of-the-way hut, out on one of the large savannahs, far from all other dwellings. She made her living by selling coffee and corn-cakes to travellers, who were always glad to rest at her hut and partake of her refreshments.

Being so far from any houses or stores, the old woman had, of course, to take a long

journey whenever she had to renew her stock of coffee, corn, and molasses. On one occasion she was returning home with a gubby or gourd of molasses, when she tripped on the root of a tree and the gubby was smashed to pieces.

The woman wailed, "See what trouble has overtaken me." She then took up the bottom of the gubby, which contained a small portion of the molasses, and with a piece of the broken vessel tried to scrape some of the precious fluid into it, all the time repeating in sorrow, "See what trouble has overtaken me." As the molasses smeared her hands, she licked it off and seemed to enjoy it.

A monkey who was hidden in the branches of the tree had seen the whole incident. He listened carefully as the woman repeated her wail, and came to the conclusion that "trouble" was the name of the precious stuff. Climbing softly down and tasting a few drops of the liquid, he decided that "trouble" was quite good, and asked the old dame where it could be obtained.

She gave him the directions and went away home.

Next day the monkey provided himself with a couple of strong canvas bags, and set out for the place she had named. Arriving there he inquired of the people where he could buy some "trouble."

At first they were surprised, but they soon determined to play a trick on him, so they directed him to a citizen who kept some fierce dogs. In the meantime they sent the man a message that the monkey wanted some trouble, and asked if he could oblige the animal.

The citizen saw the joke, took the monkey's bags into his yard, tied up a fierce bull-pup in each, and handed them back to him with the remark that he would back that trouble against any in the market.

The monkey went on his way rejoicing until he came to a place on the savannah where there was not a tree in sight, except a gru-gru palm. This, you know, is covered with terrible prickles, and could not harbour even a monkey. Here he determined to have a real good feed of trouble all by himself.

Judge of his surprise when he opened the bags and saw, not the sweet molasses, but the gleaming eyes and bare teeth of the bull-pups. They rushed at him, and you may be sure he had trouble enough to keep out of their reach, racing over the savannah, looking in vain for a tree to climb.

At last, being closely pressed, he was forced to brave the thorns of the gru-gru tree, and as soon as he reached the branches he poked his head into a Jack Spaniard's nest. If these insects did not teach him what trouble really was it is a pity.

After waiting at the foot of the tree for a whole day, hunger compelled the pups to go home. The monkey then dropped down out of the tree, and, famished, bruised, and blinded by the sting of the wasps, he wobbled on his way.

The first eatable thing he saw was a pepper-tree, and so great was his hunger that he devoured every pepper.

After that he never again wanted to buy trouble.

EXERCISES

1. Where is the "Main"? What countries do you know of there?
2. Make up another cry the old woman could have used to mean the same as "See what trouble has overtaken me."
3. Write this in another way, "She gave him the directions."
4. Why do you think the people wanted to play a trick on the monkey?
5. Why did the monkey climb the gru-gru?
6. Why did the bull-pups go home?
7. Why did the monkey eat the peppers?

LESSON 21

THE MOUNTAIN AND THE SQUIRREL

THE mountain and the squirrel
Had a quarrel,
And the former called the latter "Little prig";
Bun* replied,
"You are doubtless very big;
But all sorts of things and weather
Must be taken in together
To make up a year,
And a sphere.
And I think it no disgrace
To occupy my place.
If I'm not so large as you,

---

* *Bun,* a child's name for a squirrel.

You are not so small as I,
And not half so spry:
I'll not deny you make
A very pretty squirrel track.
Talents differ; all is well and wisely put;
If I cannot carry forests on my back,
Neither can you crack a nut."

R. W. EMERSON.

EXERCISES

1. Which is larger, a mountain or a squirrel?
2. Examine the spelling of *squirrel* and *quarrel*. What do you notice in each? Do you know any other word that ends like this?
3. Which is the silent letter in *doubt*? In *dumb*?
4. What did the mountain call the squirrel? Why did it call him so?
5. What did the squirrel think no disgrace? What did he say the mountain was useful for?
6. What could not the squirrel do? What could not the mountain do?
7. What things must be taken in together to make up the world? What to make up a year?
8. Draw the squirrel at the end of this lesson.

LESSON 22

EARTHQUAKES

THE inhabitants of the West Indies are familiar with the swaying movement of the earth, when it seems as if the building they are in had received a severe blow. Such shocks are common in all the islands, and, as you know, are termed "earthquakes."

You learned in the lesson on volcanoes that the

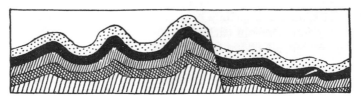

Folding and Cracking of the Earth's Crust.

earth on which we live is really a heated mass of matter in the form of a globe. Now if the interior is hot it will cool very slowly, because the rocks forming the outside or crust of the earth will tend to keep the heat in.

As the inside grows cooler it will contract or become smaller, leaving the solid crust on the outside as a shell, to fit itself upon the shrinking interior. It does this by breaking or folding, like the wrinkling of the skin on a drying "water-lemon" or "bell-apple." This movement sometimes extends for a distance of hundreds of miles. It may go on slowly and gradually, so that no sensation is felt, or it may be a sudden drop of an inch or two or even several feet.

The sudden movements are the earthquake shocks which you feel, and are, as you see, the attempts of the earth's crust to wrinkle and fold itself. It does this in certain parts of the earth more than in others, and such areas are known as "lines of weakness."

If you look at the map on page 90, you will see that the West Indies are included in the shaded part which shows these "lines."

Fortunately for us the shocks are usually slight, but occasionally one occurs which is so severe as to cause much damage and loss of life. In 1692 Port Royal, then the chief town in Jamaica, was destroyed, and in 1907 its successor, Kingston, met with a similar fate. The latter earthquake was thus described by one who was present:—

"The day opened brilliantly fine, the sun shining from a cloudless sky, and there was no indication of the coming disaster. Shortly after 2.30 p.m. a loud rumbling noise was heard, which was at first taken to be heavily laden wagons passing down the street. The rumbling became a roar, mingled with a series of loud bangs, and in a moment the whole room was shaken violently up and down, the floor rising and falling as in waves. Windows fell out, pictures came tumbling down, and all was confusion. Similar scenes were being witnessed all over the city, which long after the first shock was covered with a cloud of dust."

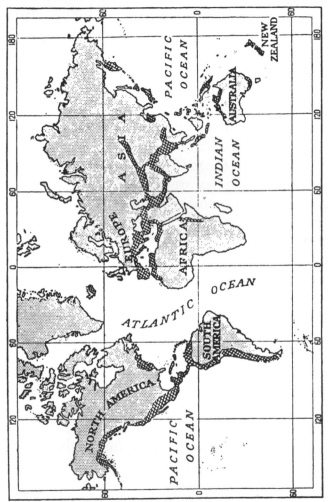

"LINES OF WEAKNESS" OR EARTHQUAKE REGIONS OF THE EARTH.

On the mainland of South America, particularly near the mountains, severe shocks are common. For this reason the houses are built with a light wooden framework fastened together with straps of leather, and they are only one storey high.

Exercise

Fill in the blanks:—

When a heated body cools it becomes smaller, and is said to _____.

The West Indies lie in a line of _____ on the earth's crust.

The shocks are not usually _____.

Low, rumbling sounds show that some _____ is taking place beneath the surface.

An earthquake is really _____ _____ _____, etc.

The effects of an Earthquake.

LESSON 23

GROUND PROVISIONS

In temperate countries English or Irish potatoes are the chief ground provision. They are not natives of the British Isles, however, but were taken there by Sir Walter Raleigh from Virginia in the southern part of North America. They do not grow well in hot countries.

In the West Indies our ground provisions are yams, sweet potatoes, eddoes, dasheen, and cassava or manioc. These take the place of English potatoes.

Yams take nearly a year to grow. They are climbing plants with small, heart-shaped leaves, except the cush-cush,* which has three-lobed ones. The stems of some, such as the Lisbon red and white yams, are smooth and winged, and often produce tiny tubers at the bases of the leaves. In the Guinea and potato yam the stems are prickly. Some yams make very large underground tubers, and others, such as the Chinese fancy or potato yam, make many small ones like the English potato.

The yams which grow wild in the West Indies are of little use as food, except the cush-cush, which is thought to have come from Jamaica. Our best kinds first came from the East Indies.

---

* "Yampa" in Belize.

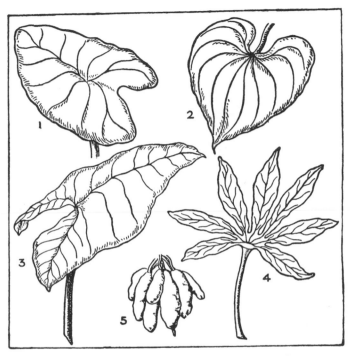

1. Dasheen Leaf.   2. Yam Leaf.   3. Tannia Leaf.
4. Cassava Leaf.   5. Cassava Root.

Sweet potatoes are largely grown in all tropical countries. There are many kinds, which are known under such local names as Red Bourbon, White Gilkes, and others. They are grown on ridges, and are vines which ramble along the ground. The underground tubers may be red, white, or yellow, and large ones weigh as much as three or four pounds. They are ready to be dug for use in four or five months.

Jamaican fruit and vegetables

There are two kinds of cassava, which you know under the names of bitter cassava and sweet cassava. Both have straight stems about four feet high, and dark green, much-divided leaves. They originally came from South America, but have been grown in the West Indies for many years.

The sweet kinds are boiled and eaten as a vegetable in the same way as other ground provisions. The bitter kinds are poisonous, and must not be used in that way. They can be grated for the purpose of making farine, starch,

Yams

or tapioca. The juice squeezed from the bitter cassava when boiled is called casareep, and is largely used in making sauces and pepper-pot.

Tannias* (or tanias), dasheen, and eddoes are all alike in habit. They are quite pretty plants, with large leaves borne on long stalks. They all make one large, central tuber with many smaller ones surrounding it.

The dasheen grows best in slowly running water, and makes the largest tubers. Eddoes and tannias are much smaller and will grow in drier places. It will be of interest for you to compare the tubers of all these and notice the difference in shape and size. There is also a difference in the leaf of the dasheen and that of the tannia. In the tannia it is divided to the stalk at one end, whilst in the dasheen it is not.

* Sometimes known as "cocoes."

In all the plants mentioned, the part we eat, which we call ground provisions, is really a storehouse of starchy food made and collected by the leaves of the plants. You should remember that the more leaves the plants make, and the more they are exposed to sun and air, the larger will be the tubers and the greater the crop.

This lesson will have taught you that while people in temperate countries generally grow only one kind of provision, the potato, we in the tropics grow many. You will also have learned the differences in habit of those we grow. Some climb, as the yam; the sweet potato runs along the ground; the cassava has a long erect stem; while tannias, dasheen, and eddoes have the greater part of their stems under the ground.

EXERCISES

1. Make a list of all the ground provisions mentioned in this lesson. How many are there?
2. Name the countries from which these plants first came —yams, cassava, potatoes, and cush-cush.
3. Draw the leaves of the dasheen and the tannia. What is the difference between them?
4. What is casareep? What is it used for?
5. What should you do to get a heavy crop from your plants?
6. Which part of the plant makes the starchy food that is stored in the tubers?

LESSON 24

FROGS AND TOADS

In Book II. you read of a class of animals called *mammals*. All animals in that group or family are alike in that they suckle their young. Now in this Book you will learn of other classes of animals which have different habits.

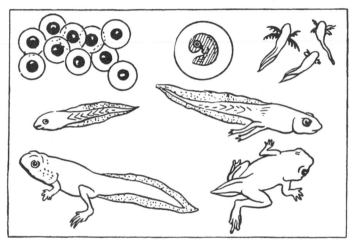

Development of Frog.

Frogs and toads (*crapaud*) are produced from spawn or eggs, which are usually laid in water. Perhaps you have seen lumps of a jelly-like substance floating on the surface of a pond. The next time you find some you should take it home or to school and keep it in water.

If you look closely you will see many tiny black specks in it. These are really the yolks of the eggs. Watch them carefully day by day, and you will be much interested in all the changes they pass through. They first hatch into little tadpoles, which are very like fishes, for they live in water and have gills with which to breathe. Later on their limbs appear, their tails and gills shrink away, and they change into frogs or toads and live on land.

Animals of this class can live both on land and under the water, and they are therefore called *amphibians*.

They are all harmless and very useful creatures,  as they devour great quantities of flies and other insects, and should therefore always be protected. Watch a frog catch an insect with its tongue, which is a

Tongue of Frog.

very curious one fixed at the front of its mouth. See how quickly it seizes its prey by this means!

Frogs have another curious habit, for as they grow they change their skin many times. The old one splits and falls off, while the new one which has grown takes its place.

There are some very interesting frogs and toads in the West Indies. The giant toad or crapaud is sometimes six inches long. He has been seen to swallow centipedes, which he seizes with his tongue, and then stuffs the free ends into his mouth with his fore feet. Unfortunately he is very fond of bees, and will stay by a hive and eat large quantities of them. He has been

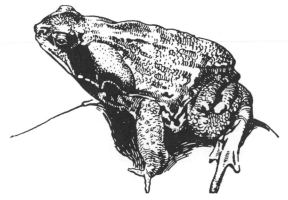

Crapaud or Giant Toad.

described as "very spotted, very like a particular style of old gentleman about the throat; very bright-eyed, very cool, and very slippy."

Others live in trees and shrubs, and are very quaint in form and beautiful in hue and these can make marvellous changes in their colours. One of them places its spawn in a folded leaf hanging over water, so that when the young tadpoles hatch, they drop into the stream.

Tree Frog.

A tiny frog which lives near running streams leaps up and catches flies very cleverly. It carries three or four of its tadpoles on its back.

Another kind, called the pipa or Surinam toad, is very rarely seen, as it lives entirely in water in some of the islands and on the Main. It is large, but has very small eyes and no tongue, and makes a faint noise like "tink."

A large frog which lives in Dominica is called Mountain Chicken, and is much sought after for the table.

Most of you have heard the unmusical concerts at night, when the different kinds of frogs and toads join in a chorus of whistles, croaks, and trills.

Exercises

1. What habits do all the frog family have?
2. Why do you think the pipa has no tongue?
3. What other creatures do you know which are amphibians?
4. Should frogs and toads be killed? Why?
5. What have you learned in this lesson about "tree-frogs"?
6. In what ways are tadpoles like fishes?
7. What is "Mountain Chicken"? Where is it eaten?
8. "Un"-musical means "not" musical. "Un"-known means "not" known. What other words do you know in which "un-" means "not"?

Pipa or Surinam Toad.
(*Photo: Dept. of Agriculture, Trinidad.*)

LESSON 25

THE DEATH OF HECTOR

In Lessons 6, 10, and 15 you read a story about Odysseus and the Cyclops. In that story you read that Odysseus after the siege of Troy wandered for ten years before he reached his home in Ithaca. The story of his wanderings was told by Homer in his poem the *Odyssey*; but Homer wrote also another poem, the *Iliad,* which tells the story of the long siege of Troy, or Ilium as it was then called.

The town of Troy was in Asia Minor, near the shore of the Dardanelles, but for many centuries nobody knew exactly where it stood.

Priam, King of Troy, had a son named Paris, who stole away the wife of a Greek king named Menelaus, and brought her to his father's city. Her name was Helen, and she was said to be the most beautiful woman in all the world.

Menelaus was full of rage when he found out that his wife had been stolen from him. At once he called his friends together; and buckling on their armour, they sailed for Troy. The Trojans refused to give up Helen, so the Greeks determined to take and burn the city.

For many years they laid siege to it, but could not overcome it. Sometimes the Trojans rushed out of their city gates and drove the Greeks away. Once they drove them to the seashore and set fire to their ships; but the Greeks always returned, and the siege went on as before.

Many brave deeds were done on both sides, and many brave men fell in the fighting. One of these brave men was Hector, the brother of Paris. He was a noble and gentle prince, but in battle he was as fierce and fearless as a lion.

One day he led the Trojans out of the city to attack the Greeks. Before he set out, however, he went to bid his wife farewell. He found her nursing his baby son.

Hector was wearing his shining helmet with scarlet feathers, and this frightened the child so much that he screamed with fear. Hector was obliged to take off his helmet before he could give his little boy a farewell kiss.

Then he bade farewell to his wife. She was afraid that he would never return, and begged him on her knees to stay at home. Hector, however, would not listen to her, but went quickly out, and at the head of his men passed through the city gates. His wife went to her own room, where she was weaving a beautiful cloth.

The Greeks were waiting for him on the plain outside, and they soon drove the Trojans back into the city. Hector was left alone outside the gates, and there he waited for a Greek prince named Achilles, who was his bitter enemy, to attack him.

As Achilles drew near, Hector's courage failed him, and he took to flight. Three times he ran round the city with his enemy close behind him.

Now Pallas Athene, a Grecian goddess, was very friendly to Achilles, and came to help him in his fight with Hector. She appeared to Hector in the form of one of his brothers, and said to him, "Surely we two can kill Achilles."

So Hector advanced bravely towards Achilles, who hurled his spear. Hector bent his head, and the spear passed over him and stuck in the ground behind him. Then Pallas Athene gave the spear back to Achilles, but Hector did not see this. He therefore hurled his spear, but it struck the shield of Achilles and did him no hurt.

Hector called to his brother, asking him for another spear, but no brother was there; and then he saw that the goddess had played a trick on him. He drew his sword and rushed upon Achilles, but all was in vain. Achilles thrust his spear through Hector's neck and slew him.

Then Achilles tied the dead body to his chariot, so that the head trailed behind in the dust, and drove off rapidly to the Grecian ships.

Now Priam and all the people of Troy were watching the fight from the walls of the city, and when they saw Hector slain a great noise of wailing and crying arose. His wife heard it, and came running to the walls just in time to see her husband's body being dragged to the Grecian ships.

THE DEATH OF HECTOR

Achilles had said that the dogs should eat the body of Hector; but Zeus, the chief of the gods of Olympus, loved the Trojans, and would not allow them to be so shamed. He therefore sent Hermes to Priam, who told him to go to Achilles and beg him to give back the body of his son.

Zeus also sent a goddess to Achilles, telling him to give it up. When, therefore, Priam was led by Hermes to the Grecian ships, Achilles accepted the rich gifts that he had brought, and gave him back the body.

For nine days the Trojans collected wood, till they had made a huge funeral pile, and on the tenth day, with weeping and wailing, they burned Hector's body upon it.

EXERCISES

1. Where was the home of Odysseus?
2. How long did he wander after the siege of Troy?
3. Where was Troy?
4. Who was the husband of Helen?
5. Who was the father of Paris?
6. Who was Hector?
7. What frightened his baby son?
8. What did his wife do when he had gone?
9. What did she fear?
10. Which goddess helped Achilles?
11. Why did Hector stop running away?
12. What did Achilles do with Hector's body?
13. When did his wife come to the walls?
14. Whom did Zeus send to Priam?
15. What did Zeus tell Achilles to do?
16. What did the Trojans do with Hector's body?

LESSON 26

OILFIELDS

HAVE you ever wondered where the gasolene or petrol used in motor-cars comes from? You may be surprised to know that it is made from an oil produced from the earth, and that large quantities of it are obtained in one of the West Indian islands—Trinidad.

It is difficult to believe that in the West Indies, where our chief products grow *above* the earth, there is one island whose most valuable product comes from *below* the surface of the earth. Yet this is so, for in the year 1958, the petroleum obtained from wells in Trinidad amounted to over five million metric tons. Its export value was £62,000,000, which was much greater than that of cocoa and sugar combined, the two main crops.

The diagram on page 108 shows how the oil collects in layers of sand deep down in the earth. There is little sign at the surface that oil is below, as the country may appear just like ordinary bush. A man who has studied rocks and soils, and is called a geologist, is employed to find spots where, if a well was sunk, oil might be expected.

Having decided on the *well-site,* or spot where the well is to be bored or drilled, the bush is cleared so that the rig or derrick can be erected. This machine works a drill, and thus bores a hole down into the ground for hundreds of feet. A space is also wanted for the boiler which supplies the rig with steam, and a good road must be made to bring the tools and the hundreds of tons of machinery and pipes.

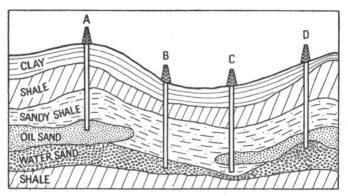

Four Wells of equal depth.
A, drilled to oil sand; B, missing oil sand; C, drilled through oil sand to shale; D, drilled through oil sand to water sand which may reduce or stop the flow. A and C are the most successful.

Fuel for the boilers is a very important matter, for the site is often far from supplies of gas or oil, and an army of men has to be employed to cut firewood to feed the ever hungry boilers.

The drilling commences; the drilling tools start to drive their way through the earth like a gimlet through a piece of wood, making a hole sometimes as wide as two feet, according to the depth the driller expects to drill.

As the hole becomes deeper the earth at the sides falls in, and large steel pipes, called "casing,"

OIL WELL.

are screwed together and lowered down the hole, thus keeping the earth from falling in and hindering the drilling.

At the start of a well the largest size casing to fit the hole is used until it is decided to use a smaller drilling tool, when a smaller size of casing is put down inside the casing already in the hole. This goes on until the hole may be only a few inches wide as it nears the oil.

One day signs of gas appear at the mouth of the well, and the smell of oil is distinctly noticed. A sample taken from the bottom of the hole shows that the oil sand which contains the oil has been reached. Drilling still continues, until suddenly the oil, forced by the gas to the top of the hole, spouts high into the air, bringing with it showers of mud and stones.

Preparations have been made to receive the oil, and the well is shut in at the top and the oil flows away through pipes to tanks or to a dam. Sometimes a well flows for a long time, but it usually stops flowing after a time, and a pump is then put into the well and the oil is pumped up. A district in which there are many wells is called an oilfield.

When the oil comes from the earth it is called *crude* oil. In some places it is thin and light, but that from other districts is thick and heavy like liquid tar.

The crude oil is pumped from the tanks to the refinery, where it goes through various processes to be separated into gasolene, kerosene, white spirit used for thinning paint, petroleum jelly, lubricating oils for machinery, and other substances.

In some cases crude oil is shipped direct to other countries in steamers specially built for carrying oil, which are known as "oil-tankers."

Exercises

1. Things found in the earth are called minerals. Plants are vegetables. Now fill in the blanks:—
      Coconut oil is a _____ oil.
      Gasolene is a _____ oil.
2. What is the difference between crude oil and refined oil?
3. Many British warships burn oil in their engines. How does it get to them from Trinidad?
4. Complete the following sentences:—
      A geologist is . . . .
      The well-site is . . . .
      Drillers are the men . . . .
      The casing is to . . . .
      A flowing well is one from which . . . .
      The following things are obtained from the crude oil: . . . .
      An oilfield is . . . .

Bringing Casing to Well by Motor Tractor.

LESSON 27

HOOKWORM DISEASE

HOOKWORM disease is a very common sickness in the West Indies, and is caused by a small worm which looks like a piece of white thread. This little worm is a parasite which lives in, and thrives on, human beings.

Hookworms

The worms lie in the bowels of the person whom they attack. They are called hookworms because the head is bent, and when they hold on to the inside of the bowels they look like small white hooks. They suck blood and also put out a poison.

If there are many worms, the person in whom they lie loses a good deal of blood and becomes pale and weak. Children become dull and slow at lessons, lazy, and not inclined to run about and take part in games. Sometimes they become swollen and short of breath in taking any exercise, and they may even stop growing.

The hookworms lay a large number of eggs, which pass out from the bowels. The eggs do not hatch in the bowels. They can only change into baby hookworms after they come out and get on to the ground.

Hookworms, much enlarged.

If the refuse from the bowels is left on the ground near houses or in places where people work or walk about with bare feet, the baby worms crawl on to the bare skin. They then bore their way in, get into the blood, and are carried into the bowels, where they become full grown and start to suck blood and lay eggs.

Hookworms attached to intestine

When the baby worms are boring through the skin, they cause that kind of sore foot called ground itch. Ground itch is the first stage of hookworm disease.

The worms may also get in by being swallowed in impure water and food. People who handle earth, and eat their food without first washing their hands, may take them in by this means.

If persons always used a proper privy or latrine like those in your school yard, there would be no eggs on the ground and no baby worms to get into our bowels. Then no one would get this troublesome disease.

Any one who has hookworm disease can be cured by a few doses of a certain medicine, so if you are always feeling tired and lazy you should go to a doctor to find out whether you have this disease.

It is very necessary to do this, for if we have hookworms, they will be constantly draining away our strength and making our bodies weak and liable to take other diseases.

Exercises

1. Fill in the blanks:—

The hookworm is a _____ which sucks _____ in the _____.

_____, _____ and _____ are signs of hookworm disease.

The young ones are formed _____ _____ _____.

The disease can be _____ by taking proper _____.

2. How do hookworms get into the body?
3. Why are they called hookworms?
4. What must we do to stamp out this common disease?
5. What is the cause of ground itch?

LESSON 28

THE WOODEN HORSE OF TROY

AFTER the death of Hector, of which you have already read, the siege of Troy still went on, and the Greeks began to think that they would never be able to take the city by force. They were a very cunning people, however, and at last they thought of a trick by which they hoped to overcome the Trojans.

Day after day the sound of hammers was heard in the Greek camp, and little by little a huge wooden horse began to rise above the heads of the soldiers. The Trojans on the city walls watched with wonder the building of the horse. It seemed to them a foolish thing for soldiers to waste their time in making a wooden horse.

At last it was finished. Then, to the great joy of the Trojans, they saw the Greeks burn their camp and sail away. Soon the watchers on the wall saw the Grecian ships fading away in the distance.

At last the siege was at an end! The Trojans, who had been kept within the city walls for ten long years, now came out in crowds on the plain, glad to be free once more to wander wherever they wished. They gathered round the strange horse, and stared at it in surprise.

Some said that it was a dangerous thing, and that they ought to beware of it. Others said that it was an idol, and jeered at the Greeks for making it. Every one had something to say about it, but at last they all agreed to drag it into the city.

The horse was hauled to the gate, but it was found to be much too large to go through the opening. They had to take down part of the city

wall before they could get the horse into the market-place.

Night came on, and the streets of the city were silent. All the people were sleeping soundly after their long years of fear and sorrow. In the market-place the great horse could be dimly seen.

Suddenly, at dead of night, a man dropped quietly out of the body of the horse. This was Odysseus. After him came many more, for the body of the wooden horse was full of the Greek heroes, and they were now in the heart of the city they had so long tried to capture.

Silently they stole to one of the gates and opened it. Outside were their comrades, who had sailed away in the day, but had returned at night. Now they trooped into the city.

The Trojans awoke, and fought fiercely against their enemies, but all in vain. The long struggle was over at last. Many of the Trojans were killed, and the city was burned to the ground. Helen was seized, and the Greek king with his beautiful wife sailed back to his home.

You can read more of the brave deeds of the Greeks and the Trojans during the siege in a little book called *Stories from the Iliad*.

EXERCISES

1. What did the Trojans watch from the city walls?
2. Why was the sound of hammers heard in the Greek camp?
3. How did the wooden horse *rise?*
4. What did the Trojans think about the horse?
5. What different things were said about the horse?
6. What did the Trojans agree to do with it?
7. What did they have to do in order to get it into the city?
8. Who first got out of the horse?

LESSON 29

SPIDERS, CENTIPEDES, AND SCORPIONS

LOOK at the pictures of the spider and the scorpion. How many legs have these animals? How many legs has the centipede in the picture? Can you count those of the millipede?

Are these creatures insects? You have learned

Spider's Web.

that an insect always has six legs. You have also learned that its body is divided into three parts—head, thorax, and abdomen. The fully-grown insect usually has wings also. You can see, therefore, that spiders, centipedes, and scorpions do not belong to this class.

They are called *jointed animals*. The head of the spider or the scorpion forms part of its body, but that of the centipede is distinct from the rest of the body. The young of most of this class are produced from eggs, and when the eggs hatch they are perfect creatures of their kind—that is, just like their parents, only smaller. Now you have learned that insects go through several changes before the perfect insect is formed.

Scorpions' eggs are hatched inside the mother's body.

All spiders have not the same number of eyes; they may have from two to eight. The spider has sharp pointed jaws, with which it bites its prey and pours in poison at the same time. In your nature-study lessons

Trap-door Spider's Nest.

your teacher will tell you how this little animal spins its thread and weaves its web to catch its prey or to make its house.

Tarantula.

The trap-door spider is a very interesting one. It makes a hole in the ground for its dwelling, and covers the top with a little door made of its threads and earth. This hole forms its hiding-place until it sets out on a hunting expedition.

Another kind with long hairy legs is often called the tarantula. It can span quite six inches with its legs. It does not often find its way into houses, but it is common in the fields. Its food consists of insects, though it is also said to eat small birds, such as humming-birds.

Scorpions are well known on account of the painful sting they can give. You can see in the picture that besides its eight legs it has a pair of nipping claws and a long jointed tail which it carries in a curve over its back. It seizes its prey with these claws and stings it to death with its tail.

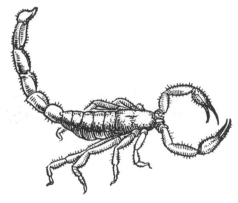

Scorpion.

They live in damp and dark places, mostly in the fields and forests, and usually hunt by night. The larger ones often eat the smaller ones. West Indian scorpions are not so large as those of Asia and Africa.

Centipedes and millipedes or congorees have long jointed bodies with one or two pairs of legs to each part. Centipedes have strong fangs in the first pair of legs, with which they can inflict painful wounds. They live on other creatures and hunt for their prey, but they seldom do much damage except to young chickens, which sometimes mistake them for a new kind of worm, and find out their error too late. Big fowls, however, can dispatch them very quickly.

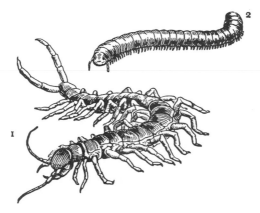

1, Centipede; 2, Millipede.

The common kind of centipede found near houses first came from Asia, and it is thought to have been brought to the West Indies in rice bags from India. It lays eggs, and sometimes a mother is found coiled round a mass of young ones. It holds on to its eggs until they hatch.

Among the native kinds is a large black one often twelve inches long. Others found in caves have legs as long as their bodies.

Millipedes or congorees are somewhat like centipedes, but are slow-moving, and have many more and hair-like legs. They are not poisonous, and are mostly scavengers, feeding on decaying vegetable matter. Congorees give off a bitter juice from their mouths, which will irritate the skin of a person on whom it alights.

EXERCISES

1. Give as many reasons as you can why spiders, centipedes, and scorpions are not insects.
2. Which of the animals mentioned in the lesson are dangerous? Are any of them useful? If so, which?
3. Draw a scorpion and a centipede.
4. In what way is a centipede like a bird?
5. Fill in the blanks:—

> A scorpion moves _____, but a _____ moves slowly.
>
> *Carnivorous* means flesh-eating. _____, _____, and _____ are carnivorous jointed animals, but _____ are not.
>
> In the _____ the head and chest are joined to form one _____.
>
> Spiders and scorpions have _____ legs, but centipedes and millipedes have _____ legs.

LESSON 30

NELSON AND THE WEST INDIES

ADMIRAL LORD NELSON, the greatest sailor in history, was intimately connected with the West Indies. When quite a young man he was the commander of Fort Charles in Jamaica, and he chose his wife and married her in Nevis.

When war broke out with France in 1803 he was in command of the British fleet, and was ordered to the Mediterranean Sea to destroy the French fleet under Admiral Villeneuve. They escaped, however; and being joined by a Spanish squadron, sailed across the Atlantic Ocean, and were pursued by Nelson to the West Indies.

The combined enemy fleet reached Martinique a week after Nelson had started, and when he arrived at Barbados he heard that they had been seen from St. Lucia standing away to the southward. He lost no time, and set off towards Tobago, and entered the Bocas at Trinidad, hoping to find Villeneuve in the Gulf of Paria.

Being disappointed, he continued his search, and proceeded north to Grenada, St. Vincent, and St. Lucia. At Dominica he learned he was only five days too late, and he continued his course to Antigua to refit his ships in the old naval dockyard there. Then in hot haste he resumed the chase back to Europe, having saved the West Indian islands from capture.

THE BATTLE OF TRAFALGAR— NELSON'S LAST FIGHT.
(*By Clarkson Stanfield R.A.*)

News travelled slowly in those days, and it was not until 20th December 1805 that tidings reached the West Indies of Lord Nelson's glorious victory over the combined fleets of France and Spain off Trafalgar on 21st October, and of his death in the hour of triumph.

NELSON AND VILLENEUVE

"Villeneuve, Villeneuve, why won't you stay?
        You've crossed the ocean o'er,
Your cruise has been long, yet you hurry away,
        when you're welcome here on shore.
Our Creole belles are worth a glance. Nay, they
        bear the palm away
O'er the daughters of France, in the song, in the
        dance—you must not say them nay.
Oh, the hours are fleet, the air is sweet, and music
        charms the ear;
Here's love and wine, and dainties fine—you
        shall not lack for cheer;
Kallaloo and *cascaradoo* and *lapp* and *morocoy* ...
Oh, life will seem an endless dream! Then haste
        to share our joy."
        Villeneuve muttered: "Od-rat, if I can!
        It's that little one-eyed, one-armed man!

"He followed me to Finisterre, he followed me
        to Spain;
Round many a reef off Teneriffe, and back to
        France again.

Then westward here to Trinidad, three thousand
     miles or more;
He haunts me on the open sea, he haunts me by
     the shore.
I have no heart for lover's part, my festal days
     are past;
To be safe back in France, alack! I'd keep an
     endless fast.
By day, by night, I strain my sight across the
     ocean wide;
'Tis an endless chase. . . . I can find no place to
     slip away and hide."
     And Villeneuve muttered: "Od-rat, if I can!
     It's that little one-eyed, one-armed man!"

So he sailed away: 'twas many a day ere the news
     to Nelson came;
Then he chased him o'er the watery floor as the
     hunter hunts his game.
The Trade Winds blew, the waters grew, endless
     the ocean spread;
The lust of battle filled their hearts as they steered
     ahead, ahead.
The tempests roared, the waters poured; Fear
     rode upon the blast;
They clapped on sail in the teeth of the gale and
     dared the desperate cast.
When the cliffs of Spain rose up through the
     rain, then the fight raged fearfully:

LORD NELSON.

Till "England's Pride," heroic, died, 'mid the
    shout of Victory.
  And Villeneuve muttered: "Save who can!
It's that little one-eyed, one-armed man!"

JUDGE RUSSELL.

(*By permission.*)

NOTES

Kallaloo, a Creole soup, the chief ingredients of which are
ochroes and crabs.

Cascaradoo, a mud fish. A local tradition is to the effect that
whoever tastes it is bound to leave his bones in the island. Usually
spelt *cascadura.* (See Lesson 14, and the poem on page 42.)

Lapp, a small wild pig.

Morocoy, a land turtle. (See lesson on "Reptiles.")

EXERCISES

1. Trace the journey of Nelson on the map on page 10.
2. Who is supposed to be speaking in the first eight lines
   of this poem?
3. How many attractions are given as reasons for the
   French admiral to stay in the Indies?
4. Did he want to meet Nelson? How do you know?
5. Who is the "little one-eyed, one-armed man"?
6. The word "fleet" is used in this lesson as a noun, and
   also as another part of speech. What is it? Why?
7. How many days did it take the news of the battle of
   Trafalgar to reach the West Indies?

LESSON 31

USEFUL FOREST TREES

WHEN Columbus came to the West Indies, there is no doubt that practically all the islands were covered with tropical forest except, perhaps, the Bahamas and parts of Barbados. In the course of time much of the forest has been cleared for plantations of various kinds, but a large section still remains.

The forests are of value in many ways. Besides producing timber, they conserve the water-supply in the soil, and thus keep the springs and rivers from drying up, and on mountains and hillsides they prevent the landslips which are often caused by tropical rainstorms falling on bare slopes.

They act as wind-belts to shelter the crops; they form breeding-grounds for the bird friends of the planter; and they even have a good effect on the climate by keeping the atmosphere damp, as you will learn in your nature-study lessons.

Lumbering on such a scale as is known in cold lands is, however, rarely possible in a tropical forest, as useful trees are seldom found close together. The reason for this is that the heat and moisture are so favourable to plants that every possible place in Nature is filled. So keen is the struggle for life among the trees, creepers, orchids, and other plants, and so dense the vegetation, that a particular tree has little chance

Logs on upper reaches of a river

to find room for its offspring near it, or for its seeds to live.

The trees which are of use are felled and the logs removed by oxen to roads, traces, or streams, and thence to the saw-mill. Despite the fact that our trees are seldom "social" beings—that is, they do not usually live together in families—the forests can supply our wants, and we need not rely as much as we do now on imported timbers. The following are a few of the most important:—

Cedar.—This tree grows to a height of 150 feet, and has large buttresses at its roots. The wood is light, strong, durable, and easy to work. It is proof against insect attack. Cigar-boxes are made of cedar, and it is the favourite wood for lining wardrobes or clothes-presses.

Green-Heart.—This tree, which yields one of the most famous woods for piles and dock-gates, is found only in Guyana. The tree grows to a height of over a hundred feet, and the timber is very durable. The lock-gates of the Panama Canal are made of green-heart.

Mahogany.—This is a beautiful tree, which in a good situation may grow to a height of a hundred feet with a trunk from four to six feet in diameter above the buttresses. Mahogany is noted for the richness of its colouring and for the beauty of its grain and figure. It is therefore considered the finest timber for cabinet-making or furniture. The original "Spanish Mahogany" of the West Indies is now difficult to obtain in large sizes; its timber is hard, heavy, and of a rich colour.

Mora.—This is one of the few "social" trees, and in Trinidad and Guyana forests of it extend over many square miles. The wood is brown, very hard, heavy, strong, tough, and durable, and somewhat difficult to work. It is suitable for ship and house building, bridges, railway wagons, and sleepers.

Purple-Heart.—As the name shows, the inner part of the tree is a dark purple. The wood is heavy, hard, strong, and durable. It is used for furniture, walking-sticks, and inlaid work.

Other useful timbers are crappo or crabwood, balata, balsam, cypre, fiddle-wood, poui, the dye-woods (log-wood and fustic), lignum vitae, locust, galba or Santa Maria, and jereton or the match-stick tree.

In some colonies clearings are planted with young trees, such as mahogany, cedar, or teak (imported from the East), so that in course of time the forests will be renewed, but more as man has arranged than on the original plan of Nature.

EXERCISES

1. "Gregarious" is a word that means to live in families. What other word do you know with a similar meaning? What gregarious tree have you read of?
2. For what purposes are forests valuable?
3. Why are useful trees seldom found together in tropical forests?

Felling a large tree.

4. What are each of the following timbers used for?—

purple-heart	cedar	fustic
mora	fiddle-wood	green-heart
mahogany	jereton	log-wood

5. If you live for forty more years, what kind of forests will you expect to see where young plantations are now?

LESSON 32

TRUE GROWTH

Introduction.—Oak trees sometimes live for many hundreds of years; but in time every oak must wither and die, and become only a dry log of wood. The lily is a beautiful flower, and is perhaps more beautiful than an oak. It is bright and shining like light. It does not live long, however; it may bloom one morning, and die before night. The poet thinks that men's lives are like oak trees and lilies. One man may live long, but his life may not be beautiful; he may be a wicked man. Another man may live for only a short time, but his life may be good and beautiful.

> IT is not growing like a tree
> In bulk, doth make man better be;
> Or standing long an oak, three hundred year,
> To fall a log at last, dry, bald, and sere;
>> A lily of a day
>> Is fairer far in May,
> Although it fall and die that night—
> It was the plant and flower of light.
> In small proportions we just beauty see;
> And in short measure life may perfect be.
>
> BEN JONSON.

NOTES

Doth make, in prose, *makes*.
An oak, like an oak.
Year, in prose, *years*.

EXERCISES

1. To what does the poet compare men's lives?
2. How long can oak trees live?
3. What is an oak when it is dead?
4. When do lilies bloom?
5. How soon may a lily die?
6. Which is more beautiful, an oak or a lily?
7. Can a long life be beautiful?
8. Can a short life be beautiful?
9. What kind of life is beautiful?
10. Divide each line into feet of two syllables, in each of which the second is stressed. Say how many of such groups there are in each line.

LESSON 33

THE SARGASSO SEA

IN the lesson on "A Voyage to London" in Book II. you read that several days after leaving the West Indies the ship encountered vast masses of yellow weed—"Gulf Weed" it is called— floating on the surface of the ocean.

This is found, as you will see by the map, in a vast eddy or central pool of the Atlantic Ocean. You know that if you throw some pieces of cork or other light substance into a vessel of water, and then give a circular motion to the liquid by

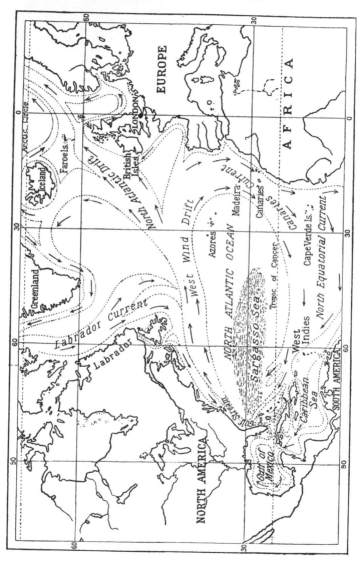

THE SARGASSO SEA.

moving it round with your hand, the fragments will be seen to form a group in the centre.

Well, the Atlantic Ocean is like the vessel, the Gulf Stream is the moving water, the Sargasso Sea the central part where the floating bodies unite, and the "Gulf Weed" the pieces of cork.

Where the weed came from originally is not really known, but it has always been there since the days of Columbus. When he entered this sea his crew very nearly mutinied, believing that the vessels had reached land and were about to run on the rocks. In this region, however, the ocean is fully four miles deep.

The "Gulf Weed" lives and multiplies as it floats on the surface, where it supports fish, crabs, cuttlefish, and molluscs.

Jules Verne, a French writer, tells us about it in a book, *Twenty Thousand Leagues under the Sea*. All boys would enjoy the adventures of the submarine described therein. He says:—

"The Sargasso Sea is a perfect lake in full Atlantic, and the waters of the great current take no less than three years to go round it. Certain authors have stated that the numerous herbs with which it is strewn are torn from the prairies of the ancient continent of Atlantis, which is supposed to have sunk below the sea there. It is more probable, however, that they are carried away from the shores of Europe and America and brought to this zone by the Gulf Stream.

"When the ships of Columbus arrived at the Sargasso Sea they sailed with difficulty amidst the weeds that impeded their course, to the great terror of their crews, and they lost three long weeks in crossing it.

"Such was the region the *Nautilus*—the submarine—was now visiting, a thick carpet of sea-wrack and tropical berries. As Captain Nemo did not wish to entangle his screw in that herby mass, he kept at a depth of some yards beneath the surface of the waves."

EXERCISES

1. Fill in the blanks:—
   Jules Verne lived in _____.
   The buried continent of _____ lies beneath the Sargasso Sea.
   The captain kept his submarine below to avoid the _____.

2. What other word could you put in the lesson instead of each of the following, so that the meaning would be the same?—

   fragments   encountered   authors
   eddy   multiplies   impeded

3. In what book can you read about life under the sea?
4. What is the "Gulf Weed"?
5. Why do you think it is called *Gulf* Weed?

Gulf Weed.

LESSON 34

THE CARIBS

WHEN Columbus arrived in the West Indies he found the islands inhabited by Caribs, whom he described as of a yellow colour, very well made with very good countenances, but with hair like horsehair.

They were a strong and healthy people; so much so that many of them lived to be a hundred years old. Yet today the race has passed away, and their only relics are a few rough rock drawings made at a time when stone implements were the only tools known. These relics have been found in St. Vincent, Guadeloupe, Puerto Rico, St. John, and other islands, always near a

Carib Idol.

waterfall. Hatchets, axes, battleaxes, chisels, and spear heads of stone have also been discovered from time to time, and here and there pottery and idols.

The women did all the hard work of their wandering life, while the men hunted, fished, and fought.

They have been described by some writers as warlike and unyielding, and by others as peaceful, gentle, mild, and affectionate. The truth appears to be that they were fierce when roused by ill-treatment, but were far from warlike or savage in ordinary circumstances.

The chiefs of the Caribs were called *caciques*. They made long voyages in *canouas*, or large canoes made from the trunk of a tree hollowed out by means of fire, and shaped by their stone

Carib Canoes.

hatchets. These canoes were from thirty to forty feet long, and often large enough to hold forty people. Each boat was governed by a captain.

They also made smaller canoes in the same way; these were called *conlialas*. They were never more than twenty feet long, and were pointed at each end. Both the *canouas* and the *conlialas* were rowed with broad paddles in the same manner, by pushing the water from them.

The men were in the habit of painting themselves with *roucou* or annatto to protect their skin from the rays of the sun, and they also used it to stain and oil their hammocks in order to preserve them from the weather.

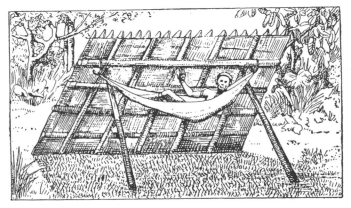

Carib Hammock.

They carried *boutous* or war clubs, and bows and arrows, which were often poisoned. Sometimes they used pieces of cotton at the end of their arrows, soaked in a liquid which burnt freely, and thus served to fire their enemies' village or houses. Their dwellings were called *ajoupas,* and being thatched, were easily set on fire by this means.

When on hunting or war expeditions they used a rough lean-to shelter against the weather, and beneath this they stretched their hammocks, which were often very beautifully woven by the women.

On great occasions the chiefs wore stone collars, often of immense weight, and armlets close to the shoulder, and rings around the leg below the knee.

Stone Collar.

Both men and women dressed their raven-black hair with great care, and the women wore bracelets and necklaces of crystal or coral which sometimes weighed six or eight pounds. Many of the young girls and married women were accustomed to wear from their childhood a kind of half stocking which extended from the ankle upwards about four inches, and another just below the knee. These were thought to be a mark of distinction.

Their amusements were the *arietoes,* or public dances, when men and women danced through the night together, accompanied by a recital of their folk-songs, and the *batoes* or ball games between two teams, in which head, elbow, and foot were freely used.

They cultivated cassava and maize or corn by using pickets and spades of hardwood.

Their government was strict obedience to their *cacique*. He was not succeeded by his son, as our king is, but by the eldest child of his sister. On the death of a *cacique* the people cut their hair and endured a fast for a month on cassava bread and water. His slaves were killed and buried with him.

Such were the original inhabitants of the West Indies, a race who were fated to die out because of the advance of the Spaniards, and to be destroyed by war, slavery, and disease, until only a few are now to be found, and these are mainly in South America.

EXERCISES

1. Carib words are printed in *italics* in this lesson. Are any of them in use to-day? If so, which?
2. Name all the parts of the body mentioned in this lesson.
3. How do you think we know all these things about the Caribs if they could not write books and have all died out now?
4. What things did they use that are still used in the West Indies?
5. Give other words for the following in the lesson: succeeded, original, countenances, relics, implements, affectionate, thatched, immense, distinction, and merged.
6. Why did the Caribs die out?
7. Which of their customs do you consider is the most interesting? Why do you think so?

Crocodiles.

LESSON 35

REPTILES

HAVE you ever handled a ground lizard or an iguana? If so, you will have noticed that it feels cold to the touch, whereas cats and dogs feel warm. This is because the blood of lizards is cold, and that of mammals is warm.

The lizard belongs to a class of animals called *reptiles,* all of which are cold-blooded. Other members of the family are snakes, crocodiles, alligators or cayman, and turtles.

These are all alike in many ways. Look at their covering. You will see that they do not have hair or fur like the warm-blooded animals, but their skins are covered with horny scales or plates. They do not feed their young on milk as mammals do, nor do they at any stage of their lives have gills with which to breathe, like frogs and toads. They breathe air by means of lungs. Young reptiles are produced from eggs.

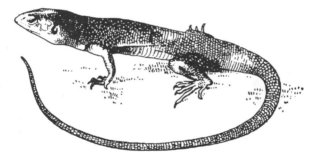

Garden Lizard.

We will now learn something of the reptiles that are found in the West Indies. Most lizards are useful as insect eaters, and they should not be destroyed. You have all seen how quickly they can run and twist and turn their bodies. The garden lizard can be found everywhere scurrying over the leaves or jumping from branch to branch of the trees. Notice how it changes its colour through all shades of green and brown to suit the surface on which it is resting.

Many trees and bushes shelter a small green or grey anole, the male of which bulges out its throat when excited. In Tobago, St. Vincent, and other islands there is a much larger anole.

The "Twenty-four Hours" is always killed at sight in the West Indies, though in Eastern countries it is never harmed. It is not poisonous,

Iguana.

as is commonly supposed. It lives in houses upon flies and other insects, and has no eyelids.

The *mat* is a very large lizard which sometimes attains a length of four feet. The large ones devour chickens and rats, but the young ones eat insects.

The iguana is a beautifully coloured green tree lizard, with a long row of soft spines on its back and a dewlap or bag on its throat. It feeds on leaves, and is sometimes five feet long.

Most lizards have four legs, but some have only two, while some which live in the earth have none at all. These are sometimes called "Two-headed Snakes".

Crocodiles and alligators or cayman live mostly in water, where they are more at home than on land. In the next lesson you will read of a fight between an alligator and a jaguar, which shows how the reptile had the advantage in the

Coral Snake.

water. They are to be found in swamps, muddy rivers, and ponds. They like to bask in the sun on the river banks, where they lay their eggs. On the Main they grow to a length of twenty feet.

There are many harmless snakes but few poisonous ones in the West Indies. Coral snakes are poisonous; fortunately they are easily known by their warning colours of red, black, and white, in belts around their bodies. They have short fixed teeth, but they rarely bite. They live in damp and dark places and feed on other snakes. Very large corals are found on the Main.

Other poisonous snakes are the bushmaster *(mapepire z'anana)* and the fer-de-lance *(mapepire barcin)*. Both of these are rough-scaled snakes, and are called pit vipers because they have a deep pit or hollow between the nostril and the eyes. Perhaps there is one of these snakes in the nature-study collection in your school; if so, examine it carefully

Fer-de-Lance.

to see this pit, as well as the long movable poison fangs which fold up in its mouth.

Another pit viper is the rattlesnake, which is found on the Main. It is a big animal, nine feet long, and very poisonous. It is called *rattle*-snake because it has a string of horny shells on its tail.

The harmless snakes vary in size, from the little glauconia, only three or four inches long, to the anaconda, often twenty feet long. The former is of the same thickness from its yellow-tipped head to its yellow-tipped tail, and it feeds on white ants and other insects. The latter lives in water, and its food consists of all kinds of animals, including six-foot alligators, sheep, and goats.

The boa constrictors (*macajuel*)[*] are common, and are harmless to man, although deadly to the smaller animals. You will learn of many of the other kinds in your nature-study lessons.

The morocoy or tortoise lives in low forest land. Several kinds, called galaps, live in swamps

Boa Constrictor.

and muddy rivers, while turtles frequent the coasts.

EXERCISES

1. In what ways are reptiles and mammals alike? In what ways are they unlike?
2. What reptiles are eaten by man?
3. How many dangerous snakes are mentioned in this lesson? What are their names?
4. Should all snakes be killed? Why, or why not?

[*] "Woulas" in Belize.

5. What is a pit viper? Give the names of some pit vipers.
6. Fill in the blanks:—

> Galaps live in ——— water, but turtles live in ———
> water.
>
> It is easy to know a coral snake by its ———.
>   This should prevent its being mistaken for a
>   ——— kind.
>
> Four kinds of sea-turtles are found in the ———
>   ———. The loggerhead has a large ———, the
> hawksbill is valuable for its ———, from which
> ornaments are made, and the leatherback is
> ———, as it is seldom seen.

Alligators.

LESSON 36

MARTIN RATTLER

I

MARTIN RATTLER was a boy, fourteen years old, broad and strong, and tall for his age. He lived in a seaport town in England, and often boarded the sailing ships at the quay to bid good-bye to his friends before they set off for the South Seas. On one occasion he was taken away on a barque, and afterwards wandered for several years in distant lands.

The ship was sailing off the coast of South America, or the Main, as we in the West Indies often call it, when it was attacked by pirates, and the crew made for the shore in boats. To avoid capture, Martin and his friend Barney swam to the beach, and found themselves alone on the borders of the huge forest which covers much of that continent.

In a very interesting book, called *Martin Rattler,* you can read of their adventures with the natives and animals. The following extracts from it tell of Martin's travels when he was alone, having been separated from Barney when he escaped from the Indians who had captured them.

II

The next day Martin resumed his travels. That night he had to encamp in a marshy place near which several alligators were swimming. In order to escape from the mosquitoes he climbed a tree and made a rough sort of sleeping place among its branches, rolling up his hammock for a pillow.

Jaguar.

As the sun was setting, and while he was looking with interest at the alligators in the reedy lake, his attention was attracted by a stealthy rustling in the bushes at the foot of the tree. Looking down, he saw a large jaguar gliding along, like a cat, towards a huge alligator that lay asleep on the bank a few yards from the water.

When the jaguar reached the edge of the bushes it paused, and then, with one tremendous spring, seized the alligator by the soft part beneath its tail. For a few seconds the huge monster struggled to reach the water, and then lay still, while the jaguar worried and tore at its tough hide with savage fury.

Martin was much surprised at the conduct of the alligator. That it could not turn its stiff body to catch the jaguar in its jaws did not surprise him, but he wondered very much to see the great reptile suffer pain so quietly. It seemed to be quite unable to move.

In a few minutes the jaguar retired a short distance. Then the alligator made a rush for the water; but the jaguar darted back and caught it again, and Martin now saw that the jaguar was actually playing with the alligator as a cat plays with a mouse before she kills it!

During one of the intervals in the combat, if we may call it by that name, the alligator almost gained the water, and in the short struggle that ensued both animals rolled down the bank and fell into the lake.

The tables were now turned. The jaguar made for the shore; but before it could reach it the alligator wheeled round, opened its tremendous jaws, and caught its enemy by the middle. There was one loud splash in the water, as the alligator's powerful tail dashed it into foam, and one awful roar of agony, which was cut suddenly short and stifled as the monster dived to the bottom with its prey; then all was silent as the grave, and a few ripples on the surface were all that remained to tell of the battle that had been fought there.

Martin remained motionless on the tree-top, thinking over the fight which he had just

Fight between Jaguar and Alligator.

witnessed, until a soft breeze which swayed the tree gently to and fro rocked him sound asleep.

Thus, day after day and week after week, did Martin Rattler wander along through the great forests, sometimes pleasantly, and at other times with more or less discomfort. He met with many strange adventures by the way.

III

One evening, as he was walking through a very beautiful country, in which were numerous small lakes and streams, he was suddenly stopped by a crashing sound in the underwood, as if some large animal were coming towards him; and he had barely time to fit an arrow to his bow when the bushes in front of him were thrust aside, and the most hideous monster that he had ever seen appeared before his eyes. It was a tapir or mountain-cow; but Martin had never heard of or seen such creatures before, although there are a good many in some parts of Brazil.

Tapir.

The tapir is a very large animal—about five or six feet long and three or four feet high. It is in appearance something between an elephant and a hog. Its nose is very long, and might almost be called its trunk. Its colour is a deep brownish-black, its tough hide is covered with a thin sprinkling of strong hairs, and its mane is thick and bristly. So thick is its hide that a bullet can scarcely pierce it; and it can push its way through thickets and bushes, however dense, without receiving a scratch. Although a very terrible animal to look at, it is, fortunately, very peaceful and timid, so that it flees from danger, and is very quick in discovering the presence of an enemy.

Sometimes it is attacked by the jaguar, which springs suddenly upon it and fastens its claws in its back; but the tapir's tough hide is not easily torn, and he gets rid of his enemy by bouncing into the tangled bushes and bursting through them, so that the jaguar is very soon *scraped* off his back.

The tapir lives as much in the water as on the land, and delights to wallow like a pig in muddy pools. It feeds entirely on vegetables, buds, fruits, and the tender shoots of trees, and always at night. During the daytime it sleeps. The Indians of Brazil are fond of its flesh, and they hunt it with spears and poisoned arrows.

But Martin knew nothing of all this, and fully expected that the dreadful creature before him would attack and kill him; for when he saw its coarse, tough-looking hide, and thought of the slender arrows with which he was armed, he felt that he had no chance, and there did not happen to be a tree near him at the time up which he could climb.

Full of despair he let fly an arrow with all his force, but the weak shaft glanced from the tapir's side without doing it the slightest damage. Then Martin turned to fly, but at the same moment the tapir did the same, to his great delight and surprise. It wheeled round with a snort, and went off crashing through the stout underwood as if it had been grass, leaving a broad track behind it.

EXERCISES

1. Complete the following sentences:—
   Martin climbed the tree because . . . .
   The jaguar seized the reptile under the tail because . . . .
   The jaguar could fight best on . . . . but the alligator had the advantage in . . . .
   Martin fell asleep when . . . .
2. What did Martin see from the tree? At what was he surprised?
3. How many animals are mentioned in this lesson? Which is the largest?
4. What words in the lesson mean the same as—injury, skin, rough, thick, swayed, ugly, combat, smothered, and margin?
5. Why did not the tapir attack Martin?
6. Is the tapir a flesh-eating or carnivorous animal?
7. Describe a fight between a jaguar and a tapir.

LESSON 37

MALARIA

DOES any one in the class remember having an illness somewhat like this?—Suddenly you felt inclined to keep quiet and to yawn and stretch your body; next a feeling of coldness came on and you began to shake and shiver and feel ill; soon afterwards your skin became warm, and the chilly feeling passed off; as you got warmer perspiration came out all over your body; then

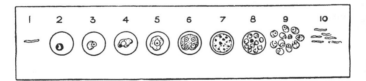

Growth and Multiplication of Malaria Parasite in
red blood-cell.

you felt better, and after a few hours you were able to go out again.

This sickness was an attack of malarial fever, and was caused by a parasite which had got into the blood and attacked the red discs or corpuscles. It is very small when it enters the corpuscle, but grows by eating the corpuscle. When full grown and still in the red disc it splits up into a number of pieces, each of which is a young parasite. The blood corpuscle then breaks up; the young parasites are set free in the blood and at once enter other red discs. The drawing will help you to understand how this goes on.

You learned in Lesson 18 that these parasites must have come from some person who was suffering from this disease. Now the important question is, how are they carried from one person to another? This is done in one way only—through the bite of a mosquito.

Malaria is not spread by breathing bad air or drinking dirty water. It is true that, if you already have the parasites in your blood, doing these things will weaken your body and will give them the chance of getting the upper hand and so bringing on malaria.

When the mosquito bites anyone suffering from malaria it sucks in the parasites with the blood. The parasites go through certain changes, and after about ten days take the form of small curved needle-like bodies which are stored in the head of the mosquito.

The next time this mosquito bites some one, these bodies—the new parasites—pass into the blood of this person, attack the red corpuscles, and give rise to malaria.

If every mosquito carried malaria, no one in the tropics could escape the disease. Fortunately, only one kind, called *anopheles,* can spread malaria. Other kinds may, however, carry several other bad diseases to man.

The malaria mosquito is found chiefly in the country during the wet season, but may live

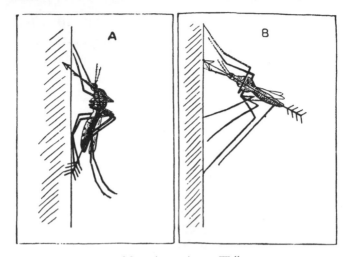

Mosquito resting on Wall.
A. non-malarial; B. malarial.

wherever there is bush and pools of water with grassy edges. It comes into houses at night, and is known by the way it rests on the wall; it stands straight out and looks as if trying to bore through the wall. The other mosquitoes which come into houses take up a different position; they look hunchbacked. You can see the difference in the picture.

The mosquito is a strange insect. When full grown it flies about, but it passes its early life in water, as you learned in Book II. It begins life as an egg, a tiny dark speck on the water, and comes out of the egg as the small worm which you see in water-barrels, and swims about in the water. Soon afterwards it changes into a pupa with a big head, and then into the mosquito which you know so well.

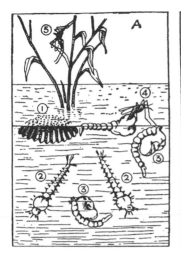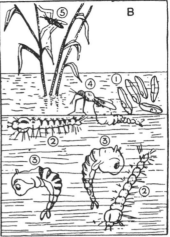

Stages in the Life of a Mosquito.
A. non-malarial; B. malarial.
1. Eggs; 2. Larva; 3. Pupa; 4. Insect emerging from pupa;
5. Perfect insect.

If we could get rid of mosquitoes we should not have malaria, as there would be no means of carrying the parasite from one person to another. To destroy every one would be very difficult, and would cost a very large sum of money. We can, however, do a good deal to protect ourselves in these ways—

(1) by filling in all pools, cutting down the bush near our houses, and removing anything which will hold water, such as pots, pans, broken bottles, calabashes, bamboo joints, old tins, and "wild pines" on the trees, so that mosquitoes may not find water in which to lay their eggs;

(2) by taking a medicine called quinine, which kills the parasite in the blood;

(3) by sleeping under a mosquito net at night, and so preventing mosquitoes from biting us.

It is important to try to prevent malaria, for even mild attacks weaken us and make us liable to get other diseases.

EXERCISES

1. Draw the two mosquitoes shown on page 160. Which one is the malara mosquito?
2. What can we do to prevent malaria?
3. Where do mosquitoes breed?
4. Broken bamboos collect water in their joints. Is it good to have them near your house? Why?
5. What causes the fever which we call malaria? Where did it come from? How did it get into our bodies?
6. What is a good medicine to take when one suffers from malaria?
7. What stages does the mosquito go through in its life?

LESSON 38

HOW TRINIDAD BECAME A BRITISH ISLAND

THREE hundred years after its discovery by Columbus, Trinidad passed from the hands of Spain into those of Britain. French privateers had been making the West Indies unpleasant for British merchantmen, and a fleet was sent to attack and destroy them.

Having succeeded in this, a few British officers and men landed in Trinidad, and a quarrel ensued between them and some of the French privateers who had reached the shore. The British were outnumbered and managed to withdraw, but next morning they landed in force and marched upon Port of Spain.

There was no bloodshed, and the quarrel was not with Spain but with France, but the incident formed one of the counts on which Spain declared war against Britain a few months afterwards, and on 12th February 1797 a formidable expedition, under the command of Sir Ralph Abercromby, set out from Martinique to capture the island.

Their task proved an easy one, as the Spaniards offered no resistance. Indeed they fired their own ships, which were lying in Chaguaramas Bay, and Apodocca, their admiral, himself helped to destroy the fleet. On the following day Abercromby landed at Port of Spain, and the Spanish governor, Chacon, surrendered the island without a fight. The destruction of the ships is described in the following verses:—

LAMENT FOR APODOCCA

Oh, Abercromby sailed the sea,
　With Harvey at his side,
Until they came to Trinity,
　Upon the weltering tide.

They sailed in at the Dragon's Mouth,
  By Madam Teteron's Rock-a,
And there in Chaguaramas Bay,
  They came on Apodocca.
      Oh, Apodocca sleeps so sound,
      Who'll waken Apodocca?

"Up, up, my lads! 'Tis broad daylight,
  This is no time for slumber;
Here be our dreaded foes in sight,
  And more than thrice our number.
'Tis vain to fly, to fight is vain;
  Was ever such a sore fix?
Their ships are all about us here,
  And twenty-four to our six."
      Oh, Apodocca slept so sound,
      Who's wakened Apodocca?

What means yon flush across the hills?
  What means yon murky veil?
'Tis not the red of immortelles,
  'Tis not the rain-clouds' trail.
The landscape fair is darkened o'er,
  The hills are in eclipse;
"To save them from our hands, my lads,
  The Spaniard's burnt his ships!"
      Oh, Apodocca's wide awake,
      You won't catch Apodocca!

What's brighter than the levin-brand?
　　What's louder than the thunder?
'Tis Spain's proud flagship blowing up,
　　Her timbers rent asunder.
She sinks, her admiral sinks with her,
　　He's flung his life away. . . .
Now he sleeps sound (as was his wont),
　　In Chaguaramas Bay!
　　　　Oh, Apodocca sleeps so sound,
　　　　Who'll waken Apodocca?

JUDGE RUSSELL.
(*By permission.*)

NOTES

Immortelles, the shade trees for cocoa. From December to February they are ablaze with vivid red flowers. (See Lesson 41.)

Madam Teteron's Rock, a small rock in the Boca Monos, one of the straits through the chain of islands which connects Trinidad with the mainland.

EXERCISES

1. What is meant by "Trinity"?
2. Why is this poem called a *lament*?
3. Who is supposed to be speaking in the second verse?
4. The apostrophe is used in the verses fourteen times to denote abbreviations, apart from indicating possession—*e.g.,* 'tis=it is; who'll=who will. Write out all the others in full.
5. By what three signs could Abercromby tell the Spaniards were destroying their ships?

LESSON 39

CORAL

WHEN you read the title of this lesson most of you will at once think of certain pink beads of a peculiar shape which you string together as necklaces or mount in rings and brooches. But that pink coral comes from one kind of coral alone, and only from a part of that kind.

Most children have learned something about how our bodies are made up. They know that inside the body there is a bony framework or skeleton, and over this frame is stretched a wonderful set of muscles, which enable us to move about. This layer of muscles is in its turn covered with paddings of fatty tissue, and outside of all is an elastic skin.

Let us now look at our distant cousin, the coral. This is not an insect, as it is often called, but it is a real living creature nevertheless. It has, however, rather different views as to the way it should grow up.

Suppose a coral could come along and watch us, to see how we live and how we are made. If our visitor could speak, one of the first remarks he would make after studying us might well be: "Dear me! What extraordinary things these humans are, and how very foolish! Fancy wearing their skeletons *inside,* and having most of themselves

CORAL.

spread over the *outside*! No wonder they have to wear clothes! And it is not only ugly, but it is stupid; one feels so much safer inside one's skeleton, especially in a well-made one like mine!"

Now the coral would probably say this because it lives almost entirely inside a very wonderful and beautiful skeleton, which serves it not only as a support and frame, but also as a very secure house. This dwelling is closely joined up to many thousands of similar houses, which do not require windows, since they also serve as clothes and screens.

The coral belongs to a race of living things that comes somewhere between sponges and molluscs, and is thus a fairly close relation to the familiar sea-egg or urchin.

It is called a "polypus" or "polyp," words which mean "many-limbed." Speaking generally, it consists of a fleshy tube usually divided lengthwise into six wedge-shaped strips, ending in a number of "feet." At the other end is a fringe or circle of threads similar to the beautiful fringes of the sea-anemones, who are near cousins of the coral.

These fleshy tubes, as they grow, build round themselves cases or homes made out of the chalk which they pick up in the sea-water in which they live. These houses of the six-room form are closely fastened together in a most interesting way. Large numbers of them form the wonderful lumps of rock that are so common in some of our West Indian islands, and in some cases even make the whole sea-shore.

You will not usually see much of cousin coral, as he is shy and does not show himself above the sea-level. What we see are the deserted houses of his family, and we must admit that these produce a very beautiful effect.

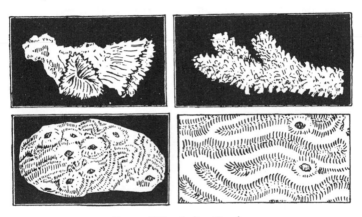

Types of West Indian Coral.

In the West Indies it is not often that we see any other than white coral, but that is very lovely. In some of the coral-producing places, however, there are corals of the most wonderful colours.

Would you like to picture the home or skeleton in which the coral lives? Suppose you had made a large number of quite flat cart-wheels, with six spokes and very small flat hubs. You could pile these one on top of the other and you would build up, step by step, a tube or house of six divisions very like the coral dwelling. There is one thing more you would have to do, and that is to bore many fine holes all along the spokes, making small passages between the adjoining rooms. All the coral family like to be able to talk and laugh together. They do not quite shut off their rooms from one another.

Now to return to the pink coral, which we mentioned in the first paragraph. When the tubes or houses are built up by the active coral, the living being, although snow-white itself, in some way stains its skeleton a bright pink or even scarlet. It also makes its hubs extra large, and it is these hubs from the deserted houses which are used to make the pink beads you know so well.

Exercises

1. What word in this lesson means the same as each of the following: house, ring, name, hues, parts, safe, being, covering, pierce?
2. In what ways is the coral different from a human being?
3. Is the coral an insect? How do you know? If not, what is it?
4. Write out the names of all the things mentioned in this lesson which live in the sea.
5. Do you know the names of any West Indian islands where coral is common?

LESSON 40

STORIES OF KING ARTHUR

I

LONG, long ago there was a great king in the island of Britain, whose name was Arthur, and whose fame went out into all the lands round about; for he was wise and brave, and the most powerful lords of his day were proud to serve under his banner.

He gathered round him a band of knights, all of whom were very brave and very noble. They loved their king and strove to be like him in thought, word, and deed.

They were all equal; no one was first, and no one was last. To show that this was so, they sat at a round table. For this reason they were known as the Knights of the Round Table.

Many were the brave deeds they did together; many were the battles they fought; many were the poor, down-trodden people they helped.

You can read the history of King Arthur and his knights in a book called *Stories of King Arthur's Knights*. The most wonderful tales are told about their doings. These stories are not all true. Indeed, many of them are nothing but fairy tales, or folk-tales, as we called them in Book I.

II

One of these stories tells us that Arthur was the son of a king, but that this was kept a secret. As a tiny baby he was given to a wizard named Merlin, who placed him in the care of a knight, and Arthur was brought up as this knight's son.

When the old king died, all the lords and knights of the land were called together to choose a new king. They met in a great church in London.

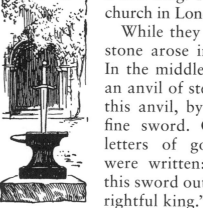

While they were at prayers a stone arose in the churchyard. In the middle of the stone was an anvil of steel, and stuck into this anvil, by the point, was a fine sword. On the stone, in letters of gold, these words were written: "Whoso pulleth this sword out of the anvil is the rightful king."

Every man who wished to be king tried to pull out the sword, but in vain. No one could do it—not even the strongest man in the land.

Now Arthur thought that the knight who took care of him was his father, and that the knight's son was his brother. He had gone with them to London when the knights were called together.

One day the boy Arthur came to the churchyard and saw the sword stuck in the anvil. At once he took it by the hilt, and drew it out of the anvil quite easily. Then he gave it to his brother, who showed it to his father. "By this sign," said the knight to Arthur, "I know that you must be king of the land. Let me see whether you can put back the sword and pull it out again."

The old knight and the two boys went to the churchyard. Arthur put back the sword into the

anvil, and drew it forth again as easily as before. Then the old knight and his son knelt down before Arthur and said, "Sir, you are king."

A great meeting of the lords and people was held, and Arthur pulled the sword out of the anvil before them all. Then the people cried, "We will have Arthur for our king!" So Arthur was crowned, and he began to choose his Knights of the Round Table. Then at their head he fought against the foes of his land, and overcame them.

THE PASSING OF KING ARTHUR.

III

One day King Arthur rode out with the wise man Merlin, and as they went along the king said, "I have no sword."

"It is no matter," said Merlin, "for a sword you shall have, and that right soon."

So they went on till they came to a great lake, and King Arthur looked out upon its broad waters and saw, to his wonder, an arm rise out from the middle of the mere. Over the arm was a sleeve of the softest silk, and the hand held aloft a sword which sparkled with a thousand lights.

"Lo!" said Merlin, "yonder is the sword of which I spoke." Then all at once they saw a fair maiden in a barge upon the lake. Swiftly she drew near to them, and stepping lightly upon the beach she bowed low before the king.

"Maiden," said Arthur, "what sword is that which is held by the arm yonder above the water? I wish it were mine, for I have no sword."

"Sir king," said the maiden, "the sword is mine; but it is appointed to be used by yourself as king of this realm."

"By my faith," said King Arthur, "I will use it as becomes a true knight and king."

"Then," said the maiden, "step into the barge and row yourself to the sword, and take it with the scabbard. And use it hereafter as you have said."

Then King Arthur and Merlin got down from their horses, and tied them to trees. And entering into the barge they came at length to the sword which was held above the water. King Arthur took it by the hilt, and the arm and hand were drawn under the surface again. Then the two men came once more to the land, but the maiden of the lake could nowhere be seen; so they mounted their horses and rode away.

King Arthur and Sir Mordred.

IV

The noble work of King Arthur was spoilt in the end by wrong and treachery, for even among the best of his knights there were traitors to their lord. One of them, Sir Mordred, led an army against him in a fierce battle and strove to kill him.

Long and fierce was the fight, and Arthur and his knights did many brave deeds. As the fight went on, Arthur's horse was killed under him, and his life was in great danger.

Then he drew the magic sword—Excalibur! It gleamed like the light of thirty torches. As he waved it, its flashing beams half blinded his foes. They could not see to strike back, and they were afraid of the strange sight.

At last the king came face to face with the traitor and pierced him through with his sword, but as Sir Mordred fell he struck King Arthur a heavy blow on the head.

The old story tells us that, as he lay dying, the king called the last of his knights, and bade him throw the magic sword into a lake. Taking up Excalibur, the knight came to the edge of the water and threw it with all his might far out into the middle of the mere.

As it fell a hand came out of the water and caught it by the hilt. Three times the sword was waved, and then it was drawn under the water.

Then Arthur said, "My end draws near. Carry me to the edge of the lake." The knight took the dying king on his back, and carried him to the shore. There they saw a barge covered with black. On the deck were three queens with crowns of gold.

Arthur was placed in the barge, and the three queens tended him gently. Then the king bade his knight farewell, and the barge moved slowly across the water. Very sad and lonely, the knight watched it disappear. He saw it—

> "Down that long water, opening on the deep
>   Somewhere far off, pass on and on, and go
>   From less to less, and vanish into light,
>   And the new sun rose bringing the new year."

Exercises

1. Give a title to each of the four parts of this lesson.
2. How did King Arthur obtain Excalibur?
3. Why was he chosen king?
4. Why do you think the title of the picture on page 174 is "The *Passing* of Arthur"?
5. Look at the picture of King Arthur on page 177. What is he dressed in? Why does he wear a metal covering? What is he holding in his right hand, and in his left?
6. What words in the lesson mean the same as: lake, damsel, ill-treated, select, kingdom, shone, disappear?
7. The picture below is a rough sketch such as an artist makes before painting a picture. Draw Arthur, the sword, and the anvil, with this as a copy.

Traveller's tree.

Cannon-ball tree.

LESSON 41

ORNAMENTAL TREES AND SHRUBS

It has been said that if we see beautiful things we shall have beautiful thoughts. We who live in the West Indies have the chance of seeing many things that are beautiful, not the least of which are our flowering trees and shrubs.

People from other lands are much charmed with the great variety and beauty of these, and visitors often come on purpose to see and to paint them. In cold countries they are not used to seeing large trees covered with brightly coloured flowers.

Charles Kingsley, who visited the West Indies in the year 1869, was a great lover of plants. In *At Last,* a book written by him about his visit, he describes in great detail the beauty of the trees and shrubs. You should read it when you are older.

In Trinidad a large tree with flame-coloured flowers clothes the hills for several months of the year. This is the immortelle. It is very widely spread, as it is the chief tree used for shading cocoa plantations.

The poui is another hillside tree which flowers two or three times during the dry season. It can be seen for miles as a patch of brilliant yellow.

On the pastures and along the streets many shade trees have been planted. Most of these have showy flowers. Amongst them are the roble, with its orange-coloured, sweetly-scented flowers, the large spreading saman, which comes from South America, and the flamboyante, an umbrella-shaped tree with bright scarlet flowers.

A pretty group of trees are the cassias. There are the pink and white-flowered apple-blossom

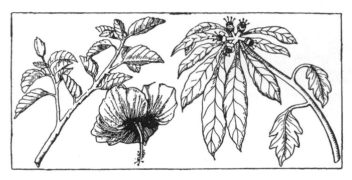

Hibiscus.   Poinsettia.

cassia, the yellow cass or Indian laburnum, and the deep pink horse cassia.

The "Queen of Flowers" or "Pride of India" gives us quite a contrast in colour. It is a big tree with large bunches of mauve flowers.

One of the most uncommon of our flowering trees is the cannon-ball. It bears its strongly scented, bright pink flowers around the trunk, and gets its name from the shape and size of the fruits.

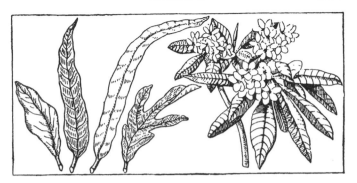

Croton Leaves.   Frangipani.

Our shrubs are not less showy than the flowering trees. Some of them with their brilliant flowers and pretty leaves are in every garden. Along the country roads we see miles of red hibiscus, which forms a neat hedge. There are many other colours of this shrub, such as white, yellow, and pink, but they are not so common.

The poinsettia is an interesting plant. It has a milky juice and is closely related to the "cactus" hedge. The brilliant scarlet parts of the plants,

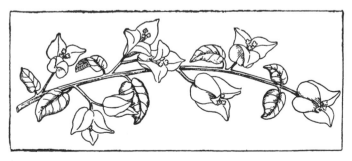

Bougainvillea.

which are at their best about Christmas time, are really coloured leaves. If you look at the plant closely you will see the tiny flowers above them.

The frangipani flowers during the dry season. There are several different kinds. One with white flowers grows wild in these islands.

Nearly every one grows bougainvilleas, and they are among our most striking plants. They all climb, but some kinds do so more than others.

Crotons, with their variously coloured leaves, and the blue plumbago are often used for making low garden hedges.

There are many other kinds of flowering trees and shrubs, most of which are as pretty as those I have mentioned.

Exercises

1. Name the colours of the following:—

frangipani	plumbago	cassias
poinsettia	roble	flamboyante
hibiscus	cannon-ball blossom	poui
croton	"Queen of Flowers"	immortelle

2. In what part of the year is each one in bloom?
3. Where can you read a good description of West Indian flowers?
4. Draw the hibiscus flower and the croton leaves.

READING TESTS AND EXERCISES

Note to Teacher.—Before Tests I. to IV. are given, the Lesson on "Making an Index" in Book II. should be revised.

TEST I

Make an index showing the names of Guyana, Belize, and all the West Indies named in this book. Which one is mentioned most frequently?

TEST II

Make an index of all the trees and plants which are mentioned in this book.

TEST III

Do the same with the animals, including fishes, insects, reptiles, and other classes.

TEST IV

What names of people are given? Make an index of them.

TEST V

Make a list of all the pictures in the book. Give titles to those which have none. Begin like this:—
"Odysseus leaving the Giants' Isle. Page 2."
. . . . Page . . .
. . . . etc.

TEST VI

Write out the words which tell you these things: give the number of the page on which they are found:—

(a) A certain vehicle was made of part of a plant.

(b) They surrounded the town for a long time.

(c) An animal was very much pleased.

(d) He made a plan.

(e) Trees help to make rain.

(f) There were many sounds from inside.

(g) Even to the horizon.

(h) The men went quietly to the entrance.

(i) Time passes quickly.

N.B.—Teachers can add to this list.

TEST VII

Rainbows

Once upon a time a Fairy met a Little Boy and said to him, "Do you know why there is thunder?"

And the Little Boy said, "Why?"

"I will tell you," said the Fairy. "It is to hammer on the two ends of the rainbow, and drive them deep into the ground, so that the bow shall stand firm in the sky."

"Really?" said the Little Boy.

"Yes, and they are driven right down through the earth into our dancing-hall, and that's the light *we* have — beautiful rainbow light, like bubbles, not just yellow like that." And the Fairy waved her wand towards the sunlight on the green hillside.

"But," said the Little Boy, "rainbows don't last long; they melt."

"Yes," said the Fairy, "and shall I tell you why that is?"

And again the Little Boy said, "Why?"

"It is because," said the Fairy, "we dig at the roots under the hill. You *can't* keep your rainbows up here. We get all of them."

EXERCISES

1. What things are necessary to produce a rainbow?
2. What are the colours of the rainbow? If you do not know, find out the next time you see a rainbow.
3. Are there any other colours besides those of the rainbow? If so, name some of them.
4. The rainbow is one of the lovely wonders of the world in which we live. Can you name any others?
5. Learn these lines:—

    The rainbow comes and goes,
    And lovely is the rose,
        The moon doth, with delight,
    Look round her when the heavens are bare,
        Waters on a starry night
    Are beautiful and fair.

6. How many separate pictures do these lines help you to see? Which do you think is the prettiest?
7. Learn these lines:—

    My heart leaps up when I behold
        A rainbow in the sky;
    So was it when my life began;
    So is it now I am a man;
    So be it when I shall grow old,
        Or let me die!

TEST VIII

A Test Picture

The picture opposite shows an unusual figure—a flying man! Where are his wings?

What does he wear? What is he carrying? What is there in his wallet?

How would you describe the expression on his face?

Why does he hold his polished shield edgeways?

Here is the description of what is happening in the picture:—

"But now came down a mighty wind, and swept him back southward towards the desert. All day long he strove against it; but even the winged sandals could not prevail. So he was forced to float down the wind all night; and when the morning dawned there was nothing to be seen save the hateful waste of sand.

"And out of the north the sandstorms rushed upon him, blood-red pillars and wreaths, blotting out the noonday sun; and Perseus fled before them lest he should be choked by the burning dust.

"At last the gale fell calm, and he tried to go northward again; but again came down the sandstorms and swept him back into the waste; and then all was calm and cloudless as before. Seven days he strove against the storms, and

INNES FRIPP.

seven days he was driven back, till he was spent with thirst and hunger, and his tongue clove to the roof of his mouth.

"Here and there he fancied that he saw a fair lake and the sunbeams shining on the water; but when he came near it vanished at his feet, and there was nought but burning sand. And if he had not been of the race of the Immortals he would have perished in the waste; but his life was strong within him because it was more than human."

Give a suitable title to this description.

How do you know Perseus was thirsty?

How was he saved from perishing in the waste?

Give other words or phrases for—the waste, he was spent, vanished, nought, blotting out, the gale.

You will find the full story of Perseus in Kingsley's *Heroes*.

TEST IX

THE PRODIGAL SON

1

A certain man had two sons: and the younger of them said to his father, "Father, give me the portion of goods that falleth to me." And he divided unto them his living.

THE PRODIGAL SON.
(*Byam Shaw.*)

And not many days after the younger son gathered all together, and took his journey into a far country, and there wasted his substance with riotous living.

And when he had spent all, there arose a mighty famine in that land; and he began to be in want. And he went and joined himself to a citizen of that country; and he sent him into his fields to feed swine. And he would fain have filled himself with the husks that the swine did eat; and no man gave unto him.

And when he came to himself, he said, "How many hired servants of my father's have bread enough and to spare, and I perish with hunger! I will arise and go to my father, and will say unto him, 'Father, I have sinned against heaven, and before thee, and am no more worthy to be called thy son: make me as one of thy hired servants.'"

2

And he arose, and came to his father. But when he was yet a great way off, his father saw him, and had compassion, and ran, and fell on his neck, and kissed him.

And the son said unto him, "Father, I have sinned against heaven, and in thy sight, and am no more worthy to be called thy son."

But the father said to his servants, "Bring forth the best robe, and put it on him; and put a ring on his hand, and shoes on his feet: and bring hither the fatted calf, and kill it; and let us eat, and be merry: for this my son was dead, and is alive again; he was lost, and is found."

And they began to be merry.

3

Now his elder son was in the field: and as he came and drew nigh to the house, he heard music and dancing. And he called one of the servants, and asked what these things meant.

And he said unto him, "Thy brother is come; and thy father hath killed the fatted calf, because he hath received him safe and sound." And he was angry, and would not go in; therefore came his father out, and entreated him.

And he answering said to his father, "Lo, these many years do I serve thee, neither transgressed I at any time thy commandment: and yet thou never gavest me a kid, that I might make merry with my friends: but as soon as this thy son was come, which hath devoured thy living, thou hast killed for him the fatted calf."

And he said unto him, "Son, thou art ever with me, and all that I have is thine. It was meet that we should make merry, and be glad: for this thy brother was dead, and is alive again; and was lost, and is found."

EXERCISES

1. Give a suitable title to each of the three parts of this story.
2. Is this story old or new?
3. Is the story told as we should tell it to-day?
4. Try to put some of the unusual phrases into words which we should use to-day, like this:—

    the portion of goods that falleth to me=that part of your property which would come to me, *or,* which will be my share.

    his living=his property, *or,* his wealth.

5. Which of the two sons is your favourite? Why?
6. Was any person in the story perfect or without any fault at all?
7. What did the father mean when he said, "this thy brother was *dead*"?
8. What is a prodigal?
9. What word or words would best describe the elder brother?
10. How can you tell from the picture on page 191 that this story was not told about people of your own country?
11. Which is the chief figure in the picture on page 191?
12. How does the artist show a contrast? How does he show that the father was a wealthy man?

TEST X

TRAVELLERS' TALES

Hundreds of years ago there was a man who wrote a book in which he told of his travels in far-off lands. He said he had seen many wonderful things; and as other people had not been with him, they could not prove that what he wrote was untrue. Let us see what some of his tales were like, and you shall say what you think of them.

1

In Egypt is the City of the Sun. In that city there is a temple made round after the shape of the Temple at Jerusalem. The priests of the temple date all their writings by the date of the fowl that is called Phœnix; and there is only one in all the world. And he comes to burn himself upon the altar of the temple at the end of five hundred years; for so long he lives.

At the end of the five hundred years the priests prepare their altar carefully, and put spices and sulphur and other things upon it that will burn lightly. Then the bird Phœnix comes and burns himself to ashes.

Now on the first day after, men find in the ashes a worm; on the second day they find a bird alive and perfectly made; and on the third day the new Phœnix flies away.

Men often see this bird flying in the country; he has a crest of feathers on his head larger than that of the peacock; his neck is yellow and his beak is coloured blue.

His wings are of a purple colour and his tail is yellow and red. He is a beautiful bird to look at against the sun, for he shines gloriously and nobly.

2

Bethlehem is a little city, long and narrow, well walled, and on each side enclosed with good ditches. Outside of the city is the Field of Flowers.

Once a fair maiden was blamed for a fault, and was doomed to die by being burnt to death; so she was led out of the city to that field.

As the fire began to burn about her, she said her prayers and asked that it might be made known to all men that she had done no wrong. When she had thus said she stepped farther into the fire; and at once it was quenched.

And the fagots that were burning became red roses; but the fagots that were not kindled became branches full of white roses. And these were the first roses, both red and white, that ever man saw. Therefore is this field called the Field of Flowers or, by some, the Field of Roses.

3

In a far country there grows a kind of fruit like a gourd; and when they are ripe, men cut them in two and find within a little beast, in flesh and bone and blood as though it were a little lamb, without wool.

And men eat both the fruit and the beast; and that is a great marvel.

I told them that in our country were trees that bear a fruit that turns into birds flying; and those that fall in the water live, and those that fall on the earth die at once.

About this they showed great wonder and some of them said it could not be true.

4

In the land of Prester John are great mountains, out of which goes a great river; and it is full of precious stones without a drop of water. But as soon as the stones enter the sea, they are lost for evermore.

Beyond that river is a great plain between the mountains. In that plain, every day at the rising of the sun, small trees begin to grow. They grow till midday, bearing fruit, but no man may take of that fruit, for it is a fairy thing.

After midday the trees decrease and enter the earth again, for at the going down of the sun they appear no more. And so they do every day; and it is a great marvel.

5

Beyond the Isles of India there is another isle, and the people of that country do not till the ground nor labour with the plough; for they do not eat anything.

They are of good colour and of fair shape according to their size, which is that of dwarfs, but not so small as pygmies.

These men live by the smell of wild apples; and when they go any distance they carry the apples with them. For if they lose the odour of the apples they die at once.

EXERCISES

1. Do you think these stories were true?
2. What year is this? What does the number mean? Were there any years before the year one? If so, how were they numbered?
3. Do you know any words beginning with *ph*?
4. What do you know about Egypt? Are there any well-known stories about that country?
5. What do you know about Bethlehem? In what book have you read of it?
6. Why were walls and ditches made round certain cities? Are there any round our cities?
7. What is the prettiest picture called up by the story of the Field of Roses?
8. Name some spices. What are they used for? Which do you like best? Which West Indian island is sometimes called the "spice island"?
9. What is a gourd? What do people make from its rind? (See Lesson 20.)
10. What do you think of the story about the river of precious stones?
11. In which of the places described would the cost of living be very cheap?
12. What do you think of the man who told these stories? What would he think of you if you could meet him now and were to tell him that people can "talk" to each other across a great ocean?